DECLARA*The*7IONS

USHERING YOU INTO THE PRESENCE OF GOD

LORRAINE LARZABAL

Accessing Freedom
Lihue, Hawaii

Cover Design: Amber Weigand-Buckley, barefacedcreativemedia.com
Interior Layout: Amber Weigand-Buckley
Copy Editors: Amber Weigand-Buckley, Douglas Jones

Editor's Note: *The Declarations* by Lorraine Larzabal are paraphrased passages that retain and convey the original meaning and essence of each Bible verse in a concise and personal manner. For each declaration, Lorraine prayerfully consulted multiple Bible versions and studied historical contexts and commentaries to capture the full meaning, richness, heart, and depth of each verse. For this reason, Scripture versions are not cited at the end of each declaration. Certain scripture citations in Chapters 13 and 16 are slightly altered by the author, such as capitalized terms for emphasis or minor rephrasing to align with the book's themes, while preserving the cited translation's intent (e.g., NIV, NKJV).

ENDORSEMENTS

"A remarkable and timely guide for affirming God's promises! It skillfully explores the roles of God, Jesus, and the Holy Spirit, leading us toward a deeper and more intimate connection with each One. As I read, I felt a growing thirst to delve further into understanding God and His presence. Lorraine's book is truly a precious gem, deeply enriching our relationship with God through elevated Bible study and prayer."

— Tracy Glass, Award-Winning and Amazon Top 100
Bestselling Author of Get Up, Girl, Let's Go!,
Certified Life Coach, Speaker, and Bible Teacher

"Lorraine is one of the most sincere and authentic individuals you will ever meet. Known for her compassion and warrior-like determination, her dedication to seeking Him and pursuing faith is remarkable. I have co-hosted several ministry workshops with her. As a seasoned minister and skilled trainer, she has guided many into profound, experiential dialogues with the Lord for years. Her '10 Steps to a Divine Encounter' is brilliant! I highly suggest you adopt this approach for your daily devotionals."

— Dr Scott Bitcon, pastor, inner healing,
deliverance, and evangelism

"*The Declarations* transforms hearts and empowers us to expect God's voice with confidence. With eighteen friends, we read sections of the declarations in unison from Chapters 1–4. We then continued through the '10 Steps to a Divine Encounter' in Chapter 15 together, thanking God aloud followed by silent confession and forgiveness. Next, we each asked Him a question we chose, writing down His responses. Several were surprised and deeply moved by their encounter and volunteered to share with the group what God spoke to their hearts. Tears flowed—Kleenex is highly recommended! What a refreshing time using *The Declarations* to discover how God values us—it's a great daily companion to my Bible!"

—LeAnn Weiss-Rupard, Best-Selling Hugs™ author
of over 7 million copies sold, and president of
Encouragement Company

"Lorraine grabbed hold of a profound truth I often share with the congregation: 'Before you can know who you are, you need to know who God is. If you know who God is, He will tell you who you are.' I regularly begin my devotion time by declaring the attributes of God. What Lorraine did was consolidate hundreds of Scriptures into a single resource, making it convenient for me to pick up the book and immediately start declaring! This is a powerful tool for all of us."

—Pastor Nathan Hanohano, Kapaa Assembly of God,
Lihue, Hawaii

"*The Declarations* leads you into the joy of giving God what He desires—intimacy through declaring His names and attributes. Lorraine Larzabal's book, with 800 first-person, present-tense scripture declarations, guides readers into His presence, fostering deep connection with His personhood. This book takes you on a continuous discovery of who God is, helping you anchor into His heart and glory. It's a life-changing tool for anyone seeking a closer relationship with the Triune God, offering a structured path to spiritual growth."

—Amber Weigand-Buckley, Multi-Award-Winning Editor and Art Director of *Leading Hearts* Magazine, Award-Winning Author and Speaker

During our annual conference, 50 attendees delved into '10 Steps to a Divine Encounter' from *The Declarations* collectively. By Step 8—asking the Lord one of the five suggested questions—participants wrote fervently, many visibly overcome with emotion. Comments included, 'I've never had the Lord speak to me in this manner before!' The book's first 12 chapters, with four each on Father God, Jesus, and Holy Spirit, deepened our conference experience. At a prayer event, many wrote 5–10 minutes of profound conversational dialogue with God, calling it transformative. We highly recommend making this remarkable structured process a lifelong tool for deepening your relationship with each member of the Trinity."

—Pastors Dennis and Rhonda Hampton, Odin Community Church, Hartville, Missouri

"I am always looking to read books that help usher me into the person and presence of Jesus—*The Declarations* does just that! This devotional is unique—over 60 readers gave exclusively 5-star praise, with nothing less, affirming many have been blessed by its powerful impact. That's because speaking out its declarations calls our spirit to attention and draws on the presence of the Lord. And the later chapters increase your understanding of what it means to have a relationship with the Triune God we serve, providing tools to grow and maintain that relationship. From the opening Scriptures to the closing prayer, this book will truly help you 'Declare your way into God's Glory!' May you be as abundantly blessed by Lorraine's book as I have."

—**Mike Van't Hul,**
Director of Network of Global Awakening,
GlobalAwakening.com

"Lorraine has gathered a treasure trove of declarations based on the Word of God, crafted through extensive hours of study. In your hands lies a book that unveils the ways and workings of our great God. As you implement the '10 Steps to a Divine Encounter,' faith will arise in your heart, unlocking the throne room of God to impact your personal, work, and ministry life. There is no greater study than the study of God, and these declarations will guide you into precisely that."

—**Timothy Svoboda,**
YWAM San Francisco Bay Area Coordinator
YWAM.org

Notes

Notes

Eternally Grateful to:

GOD . . . who makes life possible.

JESUS . . . who makes God accessible.

HOLY SPIRIT . . . who makes God tangible.

ACKNOWLEDGMENTS

I deeply express my gratitude and give glory to each member of the Trinity for Their inspiration and encouragement. They continually reminded me that the significance lies not only in completing the book but also in my transformation throughout the journey.

Creating this book was a true collaboration, with God-sent helpers beside me:

Luis, my faithful husband, who from day one believed in me and this project, provided unwavering support to bring it to fruition. He kept my office equipment running, offered his keen editing insights, gave advice, and contributed so much more. Without him, this book would not have been possible.

Jeremiah Alvarez, my wonderfully creative godson, played a key role in the book's formative beginnings, helping choose the title and shaping the front cover.

Deborah Foley, my steadfast supporter for years, provided guidance, coaching, and constant prayer, urging me to persevere with this book. She also guided decisions at key moments, spending hours on the phone helping me express God's vision for it.

Cynthia Hannan, who devoted countless hours working with me, refined concepts and clarified the purpose and impact of The Declarations.

Lucinda Teter came to pray, offer spiritual counsel, and share writing tips, guiding me through challenging stages.

Diane Mettlach, my sister, close confidante, and cheerleader, provided steadfast support throughout this journey.

Gina Kozerski and Elena Sheatz, my prayer warriors, gave constant encouragement.

My daughter Cynthia Walker joined me for several all-nighters to meet the publishing deadline.

Douglas Jones played a vital role in organizing this book, editing, and guiding me through numerous revisions.

Amber Weigand-Buckley, editor and designer, brought invaluable expertise that guided this book to completion.

THE FATHER'S MESSAGE TO YOU

In March 2023, I received this from God:

"I am calling you to proclaim these declarations to instill confidence in our relationship and offer you an unshakable assurance that I will fulfill what I have planned for your life. As you declare Who I Am, you will receive fresh revelation, bringing new life and grace, empowering you to believe for greater things as I bring heaven to earth. As you speak the declarations and fellowship with Me, I will prepare you for what lies ahead and build you so strong that not even the gates of hell will prevail against you. Listen for My voice, for I am ready to guide you on a journey revealing the depths of Who I Am in you and the potential of what I can do through you. My presence is always with you. Your Loving Father."

CONTENTS

INTRODUCTION

This book carefully presents the three Persons of the Godhead introduced throughout the Bible: God the Father, Jesus His Son, and the Holy Spirit. *The Declarations* consolidates Their names and depictions, enabling you to praise Them for Their distinct characteristics and qualities.

Call out to each of Them by Their countless names and watch what happens!

Speaking God's names and attributes not only captures your attention and focus but also God's. With ease, this practice ignites within you a sense of His awe and majesty, making Him real and palpable!

For Bible Study & Scripture Meditation—Of course, reading the declarations does not replace Bible reading. But many are reluctant to read the Bible for various reasons. They struggle to understand its numerous books and chapters and find it hard to see the relevance of God's plans and purposes in their lives. Others feel that the Bible does not adequately describe who God is in a way that resonates with them personally, making Him real to them.

Many view the Bible as primarily *about* God and His interactions with humanity, often reading it just to grasp basic events *and* teachings. Sadly, they miss the descriptive nuggets hidden throughout: the true essence of Who God really is.

The specific reference for each declaration guides you to a fuller understanding and greater revelation.

You will discover the various names, distinct characteristics, responsibilities, and unique connection each member of the Godhead shares with you. By making these declarations, you will deepen your love for God and Scripture, and be encouraged to dig in, explore Bible verses, meditate on their meaning, and their application in your life. *The Declarations is* Biblical study.

For Prayer Acceleration—Starting out in prayer by speaking the declarations opens the gates of heaven for an experiential encounter with the Lord. Expect intimacy, revelation, and inspiration. Expect a direct path to Him, quickly and powerfully. There is no more struggle in prayer, simply begin by spending a few minutes speaking His attributes from 'Who God Is.' Then, after a few minutes of thanking Him using the 'What God Does for Me' list, you will have a more reverent encounter with the Lord. Making these declarations can absolutely enrich your prayer life!

15-Minute Devotion to One Person of the Trinity— Each day, dedicate 15 minutes to speaking from the four chapters centered on one Person of the Trinity, spending about 3 to 4 minutes per chapter. Journal your insights. Alternate your focus to another Person the next day. This practice draws you into His presence, guidance, and love, empowering you with strength, purpose, and a deeper connection.

For Spiritual Warfare—When speaking declarations, you gain strength to fight the fiercest battles raging in your mind. Carefully chosen paraphrased Scriptures serve as the sword of the Spirit, spoken daily.

The sledgehammer of the spoken word crushes fear, doubt, worry, and anxiety, allowing the Lord's peace to overcome your battles. Making these declarations *is* warfare.

For Worship—Declaring 'Who God Is' and 'What God Does' for just a few minutes ushers in God's manifest presence with an anointing, like that felt after extended worship in a large church setting, resembling the glory of the Lord manifested to the Israelites (2 Chronicles 5:13-14, 7:1-3). Making these declarations *is* worship.

'10 Steps to a Divine Encounter'—Utilizing this approach, as outlined in Chapter 15, offers far more than an experience of His presence; it keys to an encounter that clears your path to clearly hear God's voice and engage in dialogue with one Person of the Trinity each day. You will discover you can converse with Them as with a friend or counselor. Engaging the 10 Steps daily will anchor you in life's storms, confirm God's work in, for, and through you, activate your calling, and align you with your purpose.

Let us include *The Declarations* to enhance and complement Bible study, prayer, daily devotion, spiritual warfare, worship, and divine encounters.

See Chapter 18 for testimonials of those using '10 Steps to a Divine Encounter' and read the 'Testimonies of People Speaking the declarations' for varied other uses of *The Declarations*!

The Trinity is presented in three categories:

God, the Father… God, the Son… God, the Holy Spirit.

For each Person of the Godhead, you will find these four separate declaration groupings:

1. **Who each One is:** *These declarations focus your attention directly and entirely on each One of the Godhead, one at a time.*

2. **What each One does:** *These declarations focus your attention on what each One of the Godhead has done, is doing, and will do.*

3. **Who each One is to me:** *These declarations focus your attention on who each One is personally to you. This will enhance and broaden your personal relationship with each Person of the Trinity.*

4. **What each One does for me:** *These declarations will expand your appreciation of how personally and actively involved each One of the Trinity has been, is, and will be.*

Each declaration is:

- Written in the first person to speak directly to each member of the Godhead, instead of *about* Them. For this reason, most declarations start with 'You are' rather than 'He is.'

- Paraphrased for personal, intimate conversation with God, rather than just speaking them into the air.

- Hand-selected and paraphrased. The list of chosen declarations includes what are considered the most impactful Scriptures, the 'meatiest' sections of the Bible related to His attributes and actions.

- Written in present tense. Most declarations have been converted to present tense. For example, the Bible states, "And my God shall supply all your need according to His riches in glory by Christ Jesus." (Phil 4:19, NKJV) This has been reworded to declare to God: You meet all my needs according to the riches of your glory in Christ Jesus.

- Certain declarations of the Godhead's traits are in lowercase for readability, such as 'You are love' and 'You are the mediator of a new covenant.'

- Written to highlight profound truths found in one part of a specific verse. For example, Jesus said, "And now, Father, glorify me in your presence with the glory I had with you before the world began." (John 17:5, NIV) To emphasize Jesus' deity, glory, and timelessness, it is rephrased to declare to Jesus: Before the world existed, You shared the glory with your Father.

The declarations are paraphrased passages that retain and convey the original meaning and essence of each Bible verse in a concise and personal manner. For each declaration, I prayed, consulted multiple Bible versions, and studied historical contexts and commentaries to capture the full meaning, richness, heart, and depth of each verse, ensuring that you can declare God's Word confidently.

I did not use specific theological terms like omnipresent, omnipotent, and omniscient, among others, in the declarations due to their absence in the Bible. However, I ensured that the attributes these terms describe were included, using terminology found in Scripture.

The three distinct Persons of the Godhead are not confined to separate roles; their roles and titles often overlap. For example, Jesus said, "Believe me that I am in the Father and the Father is in me ..." (John 14:11, NIV) Scripture often shows that the Father and Jesus share the same names, such as Lord, King, Most High, Judge, and more. They also share attributes like Holiness, as seen in these examples: the Holy Spirit's very name reflects His holiness; Jesus is the Holy One of God (John 6:69); and God's Holiness is being proclaimed unceasingly (Rev 4:8).

While the Godhead shares attributes, this book separates the names and roles of each Person to establish Their individual identities, for the purpose of fostering a closer relationship with each One and to acknowledge and honor each One.

The following is a foundational truth I learned from my pastor: Before you can know who you are, you need to know who God is. When you know who God is, God will tell you who *you* are.

This principle is shown when Jesus posed this question to His disciples: "Who do you say I am?" Simon Peter exclaimed, "You are the Messiah, the Son of the living God." Jesus immediately replied, "And I tell you that you are Peter, and on this rock . . ." (Matt 16:15–18, NIV).

Simon Peter tells Jesus who He is, which prompts Jesus to tell Peter who he is—Peter meaning 'Rock.'

You see, when you tell God who He is, He will tell you who you are.

Jesus not only identified Peter by a new name, but told him what he was called to do, promising what He would do *for* him and accomplish *through* him: ". . . on you I will build my church, and the gates of Hades will not overcome it. I will give you the keys of the kingdom of heaven; whatever you bind on earth will be bound in heaven, and whatever you loose on earth will be loosed in heaven" (Matt 16:18–19, NIV).

Jesus is asking, "What about *you*? Who do *you* say I Am?"

The Father, Son, and Holy Spirit are waiting for your answer.

1

WHO GOD IS

You are the Ancient of Days.
Daniel 7:9, 13, 22

You are the first and You are the last.
Isaiah 44:6

You are the Lord God Who Is and Who Was and Who Is to come.
Revelation 1:4, 8; 4:8

You are the Alpha and the Omega, the Beginning and the End. (You always have been and always will be)
Revelation 21:6; 1:8

You are the high and lofty One who lives in eternity.
Isaiah 57:15

You are the Living God.
Deuteronomy 5:26 and many more.

You are the Eternal King, the unseen One who never dies. You alone are God.
1 Timothy 1:17

You are the Eternal God (El Olam).
Genesis 21:33, Psalm 90:2, Isaiah 40:28

You sit in heaven on your throne, One whose appearance sparkles like jasper and sardius; and a rainbow gleaming like an emerald encircles your throne. Out from your throne come flashes of lightning and sounds and peals of thunder. And there are seven lamps of fire burning before your throne; and before your throne there is something like a sea of glass, like crystal.
Revelation 4:2-6
(The 7 lamps of fire are traditionally understood to symbolize the sevenfold attributes of the Holy Spirit associated with Isaiah 11:2)

You are the great and awesome Name (Hashem in Hebrew)!
Deuteronomy 28:58; Leviticus 24:11

You are the Creator of the ends of the earth.
Isaiah 40:28

You are God, the Father, from whom all things came and from whom all things exist.
1 Corinthians 8:6

You are the Father from whom every family in heaven and on earth derives its name.
Ephesians 3:14-15

You Are who You Are (Yahweh, I Am).
Exodus 3:14

You are the Lord (Yahweh).
Exodus 6:2, 12:12; Ezekiel 20:5

You are an Everlasting Rock.
Isaiah 26:4

You can never die (Immortal).
1 Timothy 6:16

You are the Lord God Almighty.
Revelation 19:6

You alone are God. There is no other God – there never has been, and there never will be.
Isaiah 43:10; 45:6

You are God Most High (El Elyon).
Genesis 14:19, 22

Your glory is higher than the heavens.
Psalm 113:4

You are exalted far above all gods.
Psalm 97:9

You have no equal.
Psalm 40:5

You are Holy (set apart, different, sacred).
Revelation 4:8 and many more.

Before your throne, each of the living creatures gives glory, honor, and thanks to You, the One seated on the throne Who lives forever and ever. Day and night they never stop saying, "Holy, Holy, Holy is the Lord God Almighty Who was and Who is and Who is to come!"
Revelation 4:8-10

You are the King of heaven.
Daniel 4:37

You are the great King over all the earth.
Psalm 47:2

You are the God of gods and Lord of kings.
Daniel 2:47

You are robed in splendor and armed with strength.
Isaiah 63:1; Psalm 93:1

Splendor and majesty surround You; strength and beauty are in your sanctuary.
Psalm 96:6

You are the Lord, the Holy One, Israel's Creator and King.
Isaiah 43:15

You are the Holy One of Israel.
Psalm 71:22 and many more.

You are the God of Israel (El Elohe Yisrael).
Psalm 106:48

You are the hope of Israel.
Jeremiah 14:8, 17:13

You are the Majesty in heaven.
Hebrews 8:1

You are the God of heaven and earth.
Ezra 5:11; Genesis 24:3

You are Lord of heaven and earth.
Luke 10:21; Acts 17:24; Matthew 11:25

You are the Maker of the constellations.
Job 9:9

You are the Maker of all things.
Jeremiah 51:19

You are the Father of lights.
James 1:17

You are Light, and in You there is no darkness at all.
1 John 1:5

Heaven is your throne, and the earth is your footstool.
Isaiah 66:1; Acts 7:49

You are the King of Glory.
Psalm 24:7-10

You are the Prince of princes.
Daniel 8:25

You are the Lord of Hosts (the Lord of Armies,
Jehovah-Sabaoth).
1 Samuel 1:3 and many more.

You are Lord sitting on your Throne with all the
Armies of Heaven standing near You on your right and
on your left.
1 Kings 22:19

You are enthroned between the mighty Cherubim! You alone are God of all the kingdoms of the Earth.
Isaiah 37:16

You are Almighty God (El Shaddai).
Genesis 17:1; Ezekiel 10:5; Revelation 19:15

You are the Savior.
Isaiah 43:3, 11; 1 Timothy 4:10

Mighty is your arm! Strong is your right hand!
Psalm 89:13

You are the Mighty Warrior.
Zephaniah 3:17; Exodus 15:3; Isaiah 42:13

You are a consuming fire.
Deuteronomy 4:24; Hebrews 12:29

You are the great and awesome God!
Daniel 9:4; Nehemiah 1:5

You sit on your throne. Your clothing is as white as snow, and the hair of your head like purest wool. Your throne is ablaze with flames. Its wheels a burning fire. A river of fire flows and comes out of You. Thousands upon thousands attend You and myriads upon myriads stand before You.
Daniel 7:9-10

Under your feet is something like a surface of blue lapis lazuli, as clear as the sky.
Exodus 24:10; Ezekiel 10:1

True and righteous are your judgments. Just and true are your ways.
Revelation 16:7; 15:3

You are the Lord Our Righteousness (Jehovah-Tsidkenu).
Jeremiah 33:16

You are the Rock. Your deeds are perfect. Everything You do is just and fair.
Deuteronomy 32:4

You are a righteous judge.
Psalm 7:11

You are the Judge of all the earth.
Genesis 18:25

You are love.
Deuteronomy 7:9; 1 John 4:8, 16; Romans 5:8

You are Abba, Father. (Daddy, Papa)
Mark 14:36; Romans 8:15; Galatians 4:6

You are the Father of compassion, and the God of all comfort.
2 Corinthians 1:3

You are faithful.
1 Corinthians 1:9, 10:13; Deuteronomy 7:9

You are a merciful God.
Deuteronomy 4:31; Luke 1:50, 6:36

You are a God of tender mercy.
Luke 1:78

You are a forgiving God.
Nehemiah 9:17; Luke 23:34

You are gracious and compassionate.
Nehemiah 9:17, 31; 2 Chronicles 30:9

You are good.
Ezra 3:11; Nahum 1:7; 2 Chronicles 5:13

You are slow to anger, abounding in love.
Nehemiah 9:17; Exodus 34:6

You are a God of patience and of encouragement.
Romans 15:5

Father, You are patient and kind. You do not envy or
boast. You are not proud. You do not demand your
own way. You are not easily angered. You keep no
record of wrong. You do not rejoice in injustice, but
You rejoice in the truth. You always protect, always
trust, always hope, always persevere. You never fail.
1Corinthians 13:4-8

You are rich in kindness, tolerance, and patience.
Romans 2:4

Your Word is Truth.
John 17:17; Psalm 119:160

Your voice is powerful and majestic.
Psalm 29:3-4

Your voice is like the roar of rushing waters and the earth shines with your glory.
Ezekiel 43:2

Your sound is (also) a gentle whisper.
1 Kings 19:12

Your glory is displayed in the face of Jesus Christ.
2 Corinthians 4:6

You are God Who is Peace (Jehovah-Shalom).
Judges 6:24; Hebrews 13:20

You are the God of hope.
Romans 15:13

Your statutes are trustworthy.
Psalm 19:7

You cannot lie.
Titus 1:2; Hebrews 6:18; Numbers 23:19

You do not change.
Malachi 3:6; James 1:17

You are the Lord Who is There (Jehovah-Shammah).
Ezekiel 48:35

You are a resting place.
Isaiah 28:12; Hebrews 4:10

You are the hope of all the ends of the Earth.
Psalm 65:5

You are the God of knowledge.
1 Samuel 2:3

You are a revealer of mysteries.
Daniel 2:47; Romans 16:25

You are wonderful in counsel and magnificent in wisdom.
Isaiah 28:29

You are a rich store of salvation, wisdom, and knowledge.
Isaiah 33:6

Your understanding is beyond comprehension.
Psalm 147:5; Isaiah 40:28

You are the only wise God.
Romans 16:27; 1 Timothy 1:17; Jude 1:25

Oh, the depth of the riches of your wisdom and knowledge! Your judgments are unsearchable, and your ways are incomprehensible.
Romans 11:33

You are the Sovereign Lord.
Ezekiel 12:28 and many more.

Your work is perfect.
Deuteronomy 32:4

You are the Rock.
Deuteronomy 32:4; Isaiah 51:1

Your solid foundation stands firm.
2 Timothy 2:19

You are the Potter.
Isaiah 64:8; Romans 9:21; Jeremiah 18:6

From You and through You and to You are all things.
Romans 11:36

You are over all, through all, and in all.
Ephesians 4:6

You are the Master in heaven.
Colossians 4:1; Ephesians 6:9

You are the Lord Who Provides (Jehovah-Jireh).
Genesis 22:14

You are Redeemer.
Isaiah 47:4, 48:17; Jeremiah 50:34

You are the God of Abraham, the God of Isaac, and the
God of Jacob. This is your Name forever; the Name
You are to be called from generation to generation.
Exodus 3:15

Yours, O Lord, is the Greatness, the Power, the Glory,
the Victory, and the Majesty! Everything in the
heavens and on earth is yours. Yours is the Kingdom,
and You are honored as the One Who is head over all
things!
1 Chronicles 29:11

God, this is what You proclaimed about yourself when
You descended in the form of a cloud and passed by
Moses: Yahweh! The Lord! I am compassionate and
merciful, slow to anger. I abound in love and
faithfulness, showing goodness and kindness to a
thousand generations. I forgive iniquity, rebellion, and
sin. But I do not excuse the guilty…

Exodus 34:6-7

Every knee will bow before You. Every tongue will
declare allegiance to You.

Isaiah 45:23; Romans 14:11

2

WHAT GOD DOES

You made the heavens and the earth by your great power and outstretched arm.
Jeremiah 32:17

You made the heavens, the earth, the sea, and everything that is in them.
Psalm 146:6; Acts 14:15

You gathered the wind in your hands. You bound up the waters in your cloak. You established all the ends of the earth.
Proverbs 30:4

You determine the number of the stars and call them each by name.
Psalm 147:4

You tread upon the high places of the earth.
Micah 1:3

You sit enthroned above the circle of the earth.
Isaiah 40:22

Your sovereignty rules over all.
Psalm 103:19

Your invisible qualities, your eternal power, and your divine nature can clearly be seen and understood from what has been made, so that people are without excuse for not knowing You.
Romans 1:20

Wealth and honor come from You alone, for You rule over everything. Power and might are in your hand.
1 Chronicles 29:12

You created man in your own image, male and female You created them.
Genesis 1:27

You make the winds your messengers, flames of fire your servants.
Psalm 104:4; Hebrews 1:7

You make known the end from the beginning. Your will shall be accomplished. What You speak, You shall bring to fruition; What You purpose, You shall undoubtedly fulfill. Truly You have spoken, and You shall bring it to pass.
Isaiah 46:10-11

God, your Word that goes forth from your mouth will not return to You empty but will accomplish what You desire and achieve the purpose for which You sent it.
Isaiah 55:11

What You utter, You bring to pass. When You make a promise, You keep it.
Numbers 23:19

You are enthroned on high, yet You humble yourself to behold the things in the heavens and in the earth.
Psalm 113:6

You are watching everyone closely, examining every person on earth.
Psalm 11:4

Your eyes are everywhere keeping watch on the evil and the good.
Proverbs 15:3

You cause your sun to rise on the evil and the good, and You send rain on the righteous and the unrighteous.
Matthew 5:45

You weigh the motives. You examine the heart.
Proverbs 16:2, 21:2

Your eyes search the whole earth to strengthen those whose hearts are fully committed to You.
2 Chronicles 16:9

You give wisdom to the wise and knowledge to the discerning.
Daniel 2:21

You search the heart and examine secret motives. You give all people their due rewards, according to what their deeds deserve.
Jeremiah 17:10

You speak from heaven.
Exodus 20:22

You reveal your thoughts.
Amos 4:13

You reveal deep and hidden things.
Daniel 2:22

You hide them from those who think themselves wise and clever, but reveal them to the childlike.
Matthew 11:25; Luke 10:21

You humble those who walk in pride.
Daniel 4:37

You communicate through dreams (guidance, warnings, prophecies).
Joel 2:28 (Examples: Genesis 41:25; Matthew 1:20)

You speak through visions (for the purpose of revealing yourself, your plan, to guide, to spur into action, to do something great).
Numbers 12:6 (Examples: Daniel 8:15; Acts 18:9 and many more)

You speak in righteousness.
Isaiah 63:1

You demonstrate unfailing love and bring justice and righteousness to the earth.
Jeremiah 9:24

You will by no means leave the guilty unpunished.
Nahum 1:3

You show no partiality.
Deuteronomy 10:17; Acts 10:34

You show mercy and are rich in mercy.
Matthew 5:7; Ephesians 2:4

You give good and perfect gifts.
James 1:17

You are even kind to the ungrateful and wicked.
Luke 6:35

You comfort those that are downcast.
2 Corinthians 7:6

You keep your covenant for a thousand generations
and lavish your unfailing love on those who love You
and obey your commands.
Deuteronomy 7:9; Exodus 20:6

Your love endures forever.
1 Chronicles 16:34; 2 Chronicles 5:13; Psalm 136:1

You do wonders not previously done in any nation in
all the world.
Exodus 34:10

You divided the waters before the Israelites, to gain for
yourself everlasting renown.
Isaiah 63:12

Your presence was a cloud of smoke by day and the glow of flaming fire by night.
Isaiah 4:5

You guided them to make for yourself a glorious name.
Isaiah 63:14

You parted the waters of the Jordan as You did with the Red Sea for the Israelites to pass through. You displayed your mighty hand so that all nations on earth may acknowledge your power and fear You, the Lord God, for all time.
Joshua 4:23-24

You are continually making your Name famous by performing signs and wonders around the world to this day.
Jeremiah 32:20

Your works are great and wonderful, O Lord God Almighty! Just and true are your ways, O King of the nations!
Revelation 15:3

You alone are Holy. All nations will come and worship before You, for your righteous acts have been revealed.
Revelation 15:4

Great are your purposes and mighty are your deeds.
Jeremiah 32:19

You will restore the years the locusts have eaten.
Joel 2:25

You give life to the dead and call into being that which does not exist.
Romans 4:17

You do great things too marvelous to understand; You perform countless miracles.
Job 5:9

These are just the beginning of all that You do, merely a whisper of your power.
Job 26:14

Even angels long to look into these things.
1 Peter 1:12

You place the lonely in families.
Psalm 68:6

You give power to the faint and increase the strength of the weak.
Isaiah 40:29

You heal the brokenhearted and bind up their wounds.
Psalm 147:3

You ensure that orphans and widows receive justice.
Deuteronomy 10:18

You give strength and power to your people.
Psalm 68:35

You inspire the prophets.
Revelation 22:6

You appoint apostles, prophets, evangelists, pastors, and teachers for the edification of your body (the Body of Christ).
Ephesians 4:11-12

You do nothing without first revealing your plan to your servants the prophets.
Amos 3:7

You open doors that no one can shut.
Revelation 3:7-8

You shut doors that no one can open.
Revelation 3:7

You want everyone to be saved.
1 Timothy 2:4

You were pleased to have your full nature (all of your divine essence) in your Son Jesus.
Colossians 1:19

You loved the world so much that You gave your one and only Son, so that everyone who believes in Him will not perish but have eternal life.
John 3:16

After Jesus predicted His death while in Jerusalem, He prayed to You, "Father, Glorify your Name!" And your voice, like thunder, uttered from Heaven, "I have Glorified My Name, and I will Glorify it again."
John 12:23, 28

God, it was your will that Jesus be crushed and suffer, His soul made an offering for sin, to produce many spiritual offspring and extend His days (He died but rose to life). Through Jesus, your purpose was fulfilled.
Isaiah 53:10

You did not spare your own Son but gave Him up for us all. You sent Him in the likeness of sinful flesh to be a sin offering.
Romans 8:32, 3

Through Christ, You brought the whole universe back to yourself, making peace through Jesus' blood on the cross. Thus, You reconciled to yourself all things, on earth and in heaven.
Colossians 1:20

You raised Jesus up from the dead and seated Him at your right hand in the heavenly places.
Ephesians 1:20

God, You exalted Jesus to the highest place and gave Him the Name that is greater than any other name.
Philippians 2:9

Through Jesus, and for Jesus, You created thrones, dominions, principalities, and powers.
Colossians 1:16

All your promises are "Yes" in Christ.
2 Corinthians 1:20

You are near to all who call on You; all who call out to
You in truth.
Psalm 145:18

You bless those who read aloud the words of prophecy
in the book of Revelation. You bless those who listen to
its message and obey what it says.
Revelation 1:3

You remain faithful forever.
Psalm 146:6

Your word will never fail.
Luke 1:37

You, the Ancient of Days, will arrive and pronounce
judgment in our favor, the saints of the Most High,
and the time will come for us to possess the kingdom.
The court will convene, and the enemy's dominion will
be taken away and completely destroyed forever. Then
the sovereignty, dominion, and greatness of the
kingdoms under all of heaven will be given to us, the
saints of the Most High. Your kingdom will be an
everlasting kingdom, and all rulers will serve and obey
You.
Daniel 7:22, 27

There will be no more death, sorrow, crying, or pain,
for the former things will have passed away. You
make all things new. I will write this down, for your
words are faithful and true.
Revelation 21:4-5
(Read Chapters 15 & 16, Step 9, about journaling what God says)

The new Jerusalem shines with your glory. Its radiance is like a most precious jewel, like a jasper stone, clear as crystal. The main street of your heavenly city is pure gold, as clear as glass. There is no temple because You, the Lord God the Almighty, and the Lamb, are its temple. Your city has no need of sun or moon to shine on it, because your glory illuminates the city, and the Lamb is its light. The nations will walk in your light, and the kings of the world will bring their glory and honor into it. However, no one will be allowed to enter the city except those whose names are written in the Lamb's Book of Life. There is a river with the water of life, clear as crystal, flowing from your throne and the Lamb's. It flows down the center of the main street. On each side of the river stands a tree of life. No longer will there be any curse. Your throne and the Lamb's will be within the city, and your servants will worship You. For You, Lord God, will shine on them, and they will reign forever and ever. These words are faithful and true. This will take place.
Revelation 21:11, 21-27; 22:1-6

Your throne will last forever and ever.
Psalm 45:6

3

WHO GOD IS TO ME

Even before You made the world, You loved me and chose me, in Christ, to be holy and blameless before You.
Ephesians 1:4

You are my Heavenly Father.
Matthew 5:16, 48

You are my Abba (my Daddy, my Papa).
Galatians 4:6; Romans 8:15

You know me. You know when I sit and when I stand up. You know my thoughts and are familiar with everything I do. You know what I am going to say even before I say it.
Psalm 139:1-4

You even know the number of hairs on my head.
Matthew 10:30; Luke 12:7

You are my God.
Isaiah 25:1; 41:13; Exodus 15:2; Ephesians 1:11

You alone know my heart.
1 Kings 8:39

You are my joy and my delight.
Psalm 43:4

Father, You know my heart and know what the Spirit is saying, because the Spirit pleads for me in harmony with your will.
Romans 8:27

You know me completely.
1 Corinthians 13:12

You are my Lord, my Father, and my Redeemer.
Isaiah 63:16

Your plans for me are not for adversity but for peace, well-being, and to give me a future and a hope.
Jeremiah 29:11

You are my Prince.
Acts 5:31

You are my King and my God.
Psalm 44:4

You are God, my Savior.
Luke 1:47; 1 Timothy 1:1, 2:3; Habakkuk 3:18

You are my shepherd.
Psalm 23:1

You are my reward, my exceedingly great reward.
Genesis 15:1

You are enthroned upon my praises.
Psalm 22:3

Your boundary lines mark out pleasant places for me.
Psalm 16:6

You marked out the boundaries of my land and my
appointed time in history.
Acts 17:26

And You intended that I would seek You, and
somehow reach for You, and find You. For You are
never far from me.
Acts 17:27

You are always near me, right beside me.
Acts 2:25; Psalm 16:8

You are for me.
Psalm 56:9; Romans 8:31

Nothing can separate me from your love that is in
Christ Jesus. Neither death nor life, nor any powers,
nor anything in the present or future, nor height or
depth, nor anything else in all creation.
Romans 8:38-39

You are patient with me.
2 Peter 3:9; Romans 2:4

You hear me.
Psalm 4:3; 6:9; 116:1-2

You answer me.
Psalm 3:4

You give me abundant joy when I receive what I have asked for, when I ask in your Son's name.
John 16:23-24

You hear me when I ask anything according to your will. And since I know You hear me when I make my request, I know that I already possess what I have asked of You.
1 John 5:14-15

You are the Lord my Banner (Jehovah-Nissi).
Exodus 17:15

You are my sun and shield.
Psalm 84:11

You are my song in the night.
Psalm 42:8

You are my sure foundation.
Isaiah 33:6

Father, it pleases You to make me your very own. You will not abandon me because that would dishonor your great Name.
1 Samuel 12:22

You will never forget me.
Isaiah 44:21; 49:15

You are my gardener (Keeper of the vineyard).
John 15:1

You are my protector, my keeper, and my guard.
Psalm 121:4-8

You are the God of my salvation.
Isaiah 12:2; Psalm 25:5; Micah 7:7

You are the Lord my provider.
Genesis 22:14

You are the One Who lifts my head high.
Psalm 3:3

You are the Holy One in my midst.
Hosea 11:9

You are the Lord my God Who goes before me.
Deuteronomy 1:30; Isaiah 45:2

You are my rear guard.
Isaiah 52:12

You are good to me.
Psalm 25:8; 34:8

You do not remember the sins of my youth, or my
rebellious acts. Because of your goodness You
remember me according to your loving devotion.
Psalm 25:7

You are my fortress.
Psalm 46:11

You are my protecting shield and helper and my glorious sword.
Deuteronomy 33:29

You are my deliverer.
Psalm 144:2

You are my hiding place and my shield.
Psalm 119:114

You are my shield as I take refuge in You.
Proverbs 30:5; 2 Samuel 22:31

You are my dwelling place, and your everlasting arms support me.
Deuteronomy 33:27

You are the strength of my heart, and my portion forever.
Psalm 73:26

You are my bridegroom.
Isaiah 62:5

Your name and renown are the desire of my heart.
Isaiah 26:8

You are my ever-present help in trouble.
Psalm 46:1

You are the Lord my Redeemer Who teaches me to profit (as in be fruitful, benefit).
Isaiah 48:17

In You I live, move, and have my being.
Acts 17:28

Your law is perfect, reviving my soul; your testimony
is trustworthy, making me wise. Your precepts are
right, bringing joy to my heart; your commandments
are radiant, giving light to my eyes. The fear of You is
pure, enduring forever; your judgments are true, being
altogether righteous. They are more precious than
gold, even the finest gold. They are sweeter than
honey, than honey from the comb. By them I am
warned, and a great reward is in store if I keep them.
Psalm 19:7-11

You are my healer (Jehovah-Rapha).
Deuteronomy 7:15; Exodus 15:26, 23:25

You are my help.
Psalm 121:2

You are not far from me.
Acts 17:27

You are my strong tower. I can run to You and be safe.
Proverbs 18:10

You are my refuge in the day of trouble.
Jeremiah 16:19

You are my hope.
Romans 8:24-25, 15:13

You are my judge.
James 4:12; Isaiah 33:22; Genesis 18:25

You are compassionate towards me. Your mercies
never cease. They are new every morning.
Lamentations 3:22-23

You are my lamp. You light up my darkness.
2 Samuel 22:29

You are my peace.
Hebrews 13:20; Philippians 4:9; Ephesians 2:14

You are my place of rest.
Ezekiel 34:15

You are the life and the length of my days.
Deuteronomy 30:20

You have delivered my soul from death, my eyes from
tears, my feet from stumbling. I walk before the Lord
in the land of the living.
Psalm 116:8-9

You are my inheritance.
Colossians 1:12; Psalm 16:5

You are my wisdom.
Proverbs 2:6; James 1:5

You are my rock.
1 Samuel 2:2; 2 Samuel 22:3

You long to be gracious to me.
Isaiah 30:18

God, You call me into fellowship with your Son Jesus.
1 Corinthians 1:9

You will never leave me, nor forsake me.
Deuteronomy 31:8; Joshua 1:5; Hebrews 13:5

4

WHAT GOD DOES FOR ME

You created me in your own image.
Genesis 1:26-27

You chose me in Christ to be holy and without fault even before You made the world.
Ephesians 1:4

You chose and predestined me to fulfill your plan, your purpose, and your will.
Ephesians 1:11

You called me. You are Faithful. You will do it.
1 Thessalonians 5:24

You even prepared my eternal inheritance from the creation (foundation) of the world.
Matthew 25:34

And You foreordained me for adoption as your son/daughter through Christ, in accordance with your good pleasure and will.
Ephesians 1:5

You created me in Christ for good works which You prepared beforehand.
Ephesians 2:10

You knew me in advance and chose me to become like Jesus, so that I can become His brother / sister (having Jesus as my older brother).
Romans 8:29

You call me a chosen race, a royal priesthood, a holy nation, your very own possession. I proclaim your praises, for You called me out of darkness into your wonderful light.
1 Peter 2:9

You saved me, not by the righteous deeds I have done, but according to your mercy.
Titus 3:5

You formed my innermost being, shaped my inside and outside, and wove me together in my mother's womb. So wonderfully complex! You even formed every bone in my body when You designed me in the secret place; skillfully creating me from nothing to something. You saw who You created me to be before I became me. You planned and recorded the number of my days in your book before one of them came to be. You think of me every single moment. Your thoughts towards me outnumber the grains of sand; and when I awake each morning, You are still with me.
Psalm 139:13-18

You brought me forth from my mother's womb.
Psalm 22:9

You have engraved me on the palms of your hands.
Isaiah 49:16

Father, You call me into the grace of Christ.
Galatians 1:6

You search me and point out things in me that offend
You, and You lead me along the path of everlasting
life.
Psalm 139:23-24

You are faithful and just to forgive and cleanse me
from all unrighteousness when I confess my sins to
You.
1 John 1:9

In You and through faith in You, I can come boldly and
confidently into your presence.
Ephesians 3:12

My actions will show that I belong to the truth, so I will
be confident when I stand before You. Even if my heart
condemns me, God, You are greater than my heart, and
You know everything.
1 John 3:19-20

You give me everything I need to live a godly life.
2 Peter 1:3

You establish me in Christ.
2 Corinthians 1:21

You have freely given me the gift of eternal life in Jesus Christ.
Romans 6:23

Through my Lord Jesus Christ, You give me victory over the power of sin, the law, and over the sting of death!
1 Corinthians 15:55-57

You chose to give me birth through the Word of Truth, that I would be a kind of first fruit of your creation.
James 1:18

You buried me with Christ in baptism, and with Christ I am raised to new life by faith in your power that raised Him from the dead.
Colossians 2:12

God, through the sacrifice of Christ's physical body You have now reconciled me, bringing me holy, pure, and faultless into your divine presence. And by your love and mercy, I remain steadfast in faith, firmly anchored in the truth of the Gospel.
Colossians 1:22-23

You have adopted me, and the Holy Spirit confirms this truth within my spirit.
Romans 8:15-16

You have reserved for me in heaven an inheritance that cannot be destroyed, corrupted, or changed.
1 Peter 1:4

You draw me with unfailing kindness and love me with an everlasting love.
Jeremiah 31:3

You search my heart. You examine me and know my anxious thoughts.
Psalm 139:23

You examine my heart and rejoice when You find integrity there.
1 Chronicles 29:17

You give your good Spirit to instruct me.
Nehemiah 9:20

You reward me as I earnestly seek You.
Hebrews 11:6

You will respond when I call to You and show me great and incomprehensible things that I have not known.
Jeremiah 33:3

You give me wisdom when I ask for it because You are a generous God.
James 1:5

You listen and hear me.
Malachi 3:16

You make known to me the path of life, filling me with eternal pleasures and joy in your presence.
Psalm 16:11

You are my shepherd; I have all that I need. You let me rest in green meadows; You lead me beside peaceful streams. You renew my strength. You guide me along right paths, bringing honor to your name. Even when I walk through the darkest valley, I will not be afraid, for You are close beside me. Your rod and your staff protect and comfort me. You prepare a feast for me in the presence of my enemies. You honor me by anointing my head with oil. My cup overflows with blessings. Surely your goodness and unfailing love pursue me all the days of my life, and I will live in your house forever.
Psalm 23

You are the God Who sees me (El Roi).
Genesis 16:13

People see the outward appearance, but You see my heart.
1 Samuel 16:7

You grant favor and honor. You do not withhold good things from me when I walk with integrity.
Psalm 84:11

You do not want me to worship any other gods, for You are a jealous God, and your name is Jealous.
Exodus 34:14

You daily bear my burdens.
Psalm 68:19

You take care of me as I continually give my burdens
to You. You will not permit the righteous to be moved.
Psalm 55:22

You comfort me in all my troubles so that I can comfort
others. When they are troubled, I will be able to give
them the same comfort You have given me.
2 Corinthians 1:4

You show me great mercy.
Romans 12:1

Father, your grace is sufficient for me, for your power
is perfected in my weaknesses, insults, hardships,
persecutions, and difficulties. For You are strong when
I am weak.
2 Corinthians 12:9-10

Your kindness and patience lead me to repentance.
Romans 2:4

You discipline me for my good in order that I may
share in your holiness. Being trained by your discipline
produces in me a harvest of righteousness and peace.
Hebrews 12:10-11

You always cause me to triumph in You and use me to
spread the knowledge of You everywhere, like sweet
perfume.
2 Corinthians 2:14

You give me songs in the night.
Psalm 42:8

You are with me when I pass through the waters; and when I go through the rivers, they do not overwhelm me. When I walk through the fire, I am not scorched.
Isaiah 43:2

Just as gold is tested for purity by fire, and silver is refined by fire, so through fire You purify and refine me.
Zechariah 13:9

You prune me when I bear fruit to make me even more fruitful.
John 15:2

Your fire reveals and tests the quality and value of my work.
1 Corinthians 3:13

You will bless me if I do not give up when my faith is being tested.
James 1:12

You have planted eternity in my heart.
Ecclesiastes 3:11

You bless me and keep me; your face shines upon me and you are gracious to me; You turn your face toward me and give me peace.
Numbers 6:24-25

You lead me to a place of safety. You rescue me because You delight in me.
2 Samuel 22:20; Psalm 18:19

You rescue me from every trap and protect me from deadly disease. You cover me with your feathers and under your wings I find refuge; your faithfulness is my protective shield. You command your angels to defend and guard me in all my ways. You answer me when I call. You deliver me and honor me. With long life You satisfy me and show me your salvation.
Psalm 91:3-4, 11, 15-16

In the day of trouble, You hide me in your tabernacle; in the secret place of your sanctuary and hold my head high above my enemies around me.
Psalm 27:5-6

You send your terror ahead of me and throw into confusion every enemy I encounter. You make all my enemies turn their backs and run.
Exodus 23:27

You redeem my soul out of all adversity.
1 Kings 1:29

You surround me with songs of deliverance.
Psalm 32:7

You deliver me out of all my afflictions.
Psalm 34:19

Even though many oppose me, You rescue me unharmed from the battles that wage against me.
Psalm 55:18

Little by little You drive out my enemies before me, until I increase enough to take possession of my land.
Exodus 23:30

You plead my case and take vengeance on my behalf.
Jeremiah 51:36

You laugh when the wicked plot against me, for You know their day is coming.
Psalm 37:13

You rejoice over me with singing.
Zephaniah 3:17

You lift me up from the gates of death.
Psalm 9:13

You take hold of my right hand and say, "Do not fear, I will help you."
Isaiah 41:13

You ride upon the heavens to help me.
Deuteronomy 33:26

You are using my sufferings to restore, establish, and strengthen me.
1 Peter 5:10

You are with me when my spirit is contrite and humble. You restore me when my spirit is crushed and revive my courage as I come to You with a repentant heart.
Isaiah 57:15

You are close to the brokenhearted.
Psalm 34:18

You save those who are crushed in spirit.
Psalm 34:18

Father, You love me as much as You love Jesus.
John 17:23

You crown me with loving kindness and tender mercies.
Psalm 103:4

You rejoice over me as a bridegroom rejoices over his bride; You marry me just as a young man marries a young woman.
Isaiah 62:5

You call me by a new name; "My Delight is in You" and "The Bride of God." I am no longer called deserted, or forsaken.
Isaiah 62:4

You redeemed me, called me by name: I am yours.
Isaiah 43:1

You sanctify me.
John 17:19

You bless me abundantly, that in all things, at all times, having all that I need, I abound in every good work.
2 Corinthians 9:8

You equip me with all I need for doing your will. And through the power of Jesus Christ, You accomplish in me every good thing that is pleasing to You.
Hebrews 13:21

You are working in me, giving me the desire and the power to do what pleases You.
Philippians 2:13

You will fulfill your purpose for me.
Psalm 57:2; 138:8

Father, You are watching over your Word to accomplish it in my life.
Jeremiah 1:12

All Scripture is God-breathed and is useful to teach me what is true and to make me realize what is wrong in my life. Your Word corrects me when I am wrong and teaches me to do what is right. Your Word prepares and equips me to do every good work.
2 Timothy 3:16-17

You work all things for my good.
Romans 8:28

You began a good work in me, and You will carry it on to completion until the day of Christ Jesus.
Philippians 1:6

You placed your seal on me and put your Spirit in my heart as a pledge for what is to come.
2 Corinthians 1:22; Ephesians 1:13-14

You do not turn away my prayer.
Psalm 66:20

You forgive me as I forgive others.
Matthew 6:14-15; Mark 11:25-26; Luke 11:4; John 20:23

You heal all my diseases.
Psalm 103:3; Exodus 15:26

You restore me to health and heal my wounds.
Jeremiah 30:17

You bless my food and water, and as I serve You and cast away idols, You remove sickness from me.
Exodus 23:24-25

There will be no miscarriages or barrenness, and You grant me a full life span.
Exodus 23:26

You sent your Word and healed me; You rescued me from the grave.
Psalm 107:20

You broke away my chains.
Psalm 107:14

You will raise me from the dead by your power, just as You raised Jesus from the dead.
1 Corinthians 6:14

You satisfy my mouth with good things.
Psalm 103:5

Father, this is an everlasting covenant You have with me: that You will never stop doing good for me.
Jeremiah 32:40

You keep track of all my sorrows and collect all my tears in your bottle. You record each one in your book.
Psalm 56:8

You meet all my needs according to the riches of your glory in Christ Jesus.
Philippians 4:19

You instruct me to not put my hope in the uncertainty of wealth, but to put my hope in You, Who richly provides all things for me to enjoy.
1 Timothy 6:17

You go before me, and You are with me; You will never leave me.
Deuteronomy 31:8

You keep me in perfect peace as I trust in You and fix my thoughts on You.
Isaiah 26:3

You keep me from stumbling and with great joy You will present me, faultless, before your glorious presence.
Jude 1:24

You do immeasurably more than all I ask or imagine, according to your power that is at work within me.
Ephesians 3:20

Father, You will sanctify me entirely that my spirit,
soul, and body be preserved complete, without blame
at the return of your Son Jesus.
1 Thessalonians 5:23

You called me. You are faithful. You will do it.
1 Thessalonians 5:24

You will soon crush Satan under my feet.
Romans 16:20

You will wipe away every tear from my eyes.
Revelation 7:17

You will give me a new name if I choose what pleases
You and hold fast to your covenant. My new
everlasting name will not be cut off.
Isaiah 56:5

Your own mouth will give me a new name and
You will hold me in your hand for all to see – a
splendid crown in the palm of your hand.
Isaiah 62:2-3

5

WHO JESUS IS

You are the beginning. You existed before anything
else.
Colossians 1:17-18

You are One whose origin is from of old, from ancient
times.
Micah 5:2

You are the Word.
John 1:14

You were in the beginning with God, as the Word, and
You are God.
John 1:1-2

You are and You were, and You are to come.
Revelation 1:8

You and the Father are one.
John 10:30

Before the world existed, You shared the glory with
your Father.
John 17:5

Through You, God made the universe.
Hebrews 1:2; John 1:10

You sit at the right hand of the throne of the Majesty in the heavens.
Ephesians 1:20; Hebrews 8:1; Acts 7:55

Through You, everything was made, and nothing was created except through You.
John 1:3

You are the Originator of the creation of God.
Revelation 3:14

Through You and for You all things were created: things in heaven and on earth, visible and invisible.
Colossians 1:16

You are Lord, through whom all things came and through whom all things exist.
1 Corinthians 8:6

Your appearance is of a man upon your throne. Your throne is of sapphire stone. A color of amber, and the appearance of fire is round about and within You. Your loins have the appearance of fire and brilliant light surrounds You. Your glory is the likeness of a rainbow appearing as radiant light all around You.
Ezekiel 1:26-28

Your clothing is fragrant with myrrh and aloes and cassia.
Psalm 45:8

You are the wisdom of God.
1 Corinthians 1:24

In You all the treasures of wisdom and knowledge are
hidden.
Colossians 2:3

You are before Abraham was born.
(before Abraham was born, I Am)
John 8:58

You are a descendant of King David, and of Abraham.
Matthew 1:1

You are called Immanuel, God with us.
Isaiah 7:14; Matthew 1:23

You are God's Son from heaven.
1 Thessalonians 1:10

You are the stairway connecting an open heaven to
earth, upon whom angels ascend and descend.
John 1:51; Genesis 28:12

You are the Living Bread that came down from heaven,
the bread of God, the true bread, the bread of life.
John 6:32-33, 48, 51

You (the manna) were the Israelites' spiritual food.
1 Corinthians 10:3-5

You increased in wisdom and stature, and in favor
with God and man.
Luke 4:52

You are strong in spirit, filled with wisdom, and the grace of God is upon You.
Luke 2:40

God gave You the fullness of His Spirit.
John 3:34

You fill all in all.
Ephesians 1:23

You are the image of the invisible God.
Colossians 1:15

In You, all the fullness of God is alive in bodily form.
Colossians 2:9

Jesus, You are the radiance of God's glory and the exact representation of God's nature.
Hebrews 1:3

Your glory is seen, the glory of the One and only Son, Who came from the Father, full of grace and truth.
John 1:14

Your face shines with the light of the knowledge of the glory of God.
2 Corinthians 4:6

You shine with the glory of God. Your radiance is like a most precious jewel, like a jasper stone, clear as crystal.
Revelation 21:11

On You, Jesus, God placed His seal of approval.
John 6:27

You are in the Father and the Father is in You.
John 14:10

God spoke to You audibly (both at your baptism and at your transfiguration) saying, "You are My beloved Son, in whom I love; in You I am well pleased!"
Matthew 3:17, 17:5; Mark 1:11; Luke 3:22; 2 Peter 1:17

You are the Holy One of God.
John 6:69; Luke 4:34

You are holy, innocent, undefiled, set apart from sinners, and exalted above the heavens!
Hebrews 7:26

You are the Anointed One.
Psalm 2:2; Acts 4:26

You are the Christ (the Anointed One, Messiah).
Luke 9:20; Matthew 16:16 and many more.

You are Truth.
John 14:6

You are the power of God.
1 Corinthians 1:24

You are head over every ruler and authority.
Colossians 2:10

Jesus, You stand among the seven golden lampstands, dressed in a robe reaching down to your feet, with a golden sash around your chest. The hair on your head is as white as snow, and your eyes are like blazing fire. Your feet are like bronze glowing in a furnace, and your voice is like the sound of rushing waters. In your right hand, You hold seven stars, and coming out of your mouth is a sharp, double-edged sword (the word of God, the sword of the Spirit). Your face is like the sun shining in all its brilliance.

Revelation 1:12-16
(Verse 20 explains that the seven lampstands are the seven churches, and the seven stars are the angels of the seven churches)

You are the heavenly man.
1 Corinthians 15:44-49

You are the bright Morning Star.
Revelation 22:16

You are the True Light.
1 John 2:8; John 1:9

You are a light revealing God to the nations.
Luke 2:32; Acts 13:47; Isaiah 42:6

You are the Light of the World.
John 3:19, 8:12, 9:5

You are a great light to those living in darkness; on those living in the shadow of death.
Isaiah 9:2; John 12:46; Matthew 4:16

You are the Way, the Truth, and the Life.
John 14:6

You are the Author of Life.
Acts 3:15

You are the Word of Life.
1 John 1:1

You are called Wonderful Counselor, Mighty God,
Everlasting Father, Prince of Peace.
Isaiah 9:6

You are Jesus, Son of the Most High God.
Mark 5:7

You are gentle and humble in Spirit.
Matthew 11:29

You are the Son whom God loves.
Colossians 1:13

You are the beloved One.
Ephesians 1:6

You are heir of all things.
Hebrews 1:2

You were given the highest place of honor in heaven.
Philippians 2:9

You are the Lion from the tribe of Judah.
Revelation 5:5

You are the Son of God.
Luke 1:35 and many more.

You are the Christ, the Son of the Blessed.
Mark 14:61-62

You are I Am.
John 8:24, 28, 58; 18:6

You are the Son of Man.
Matthew 24:30 and many more.

You are supreme over all creation.
Colossians 1:15

The government rests on your shoulders.
Isaiah 9:6

You are the Nazarene.
Mark 14:67; 16:6

You are Jesus of Nazareth.
Acts 2:22; 4:10

You are King of the Jews.
Matthew 27:37 and many more.

You are the King of Israel.
Mark 15:32

You are the Lamb in the center of God's throne.
Revelation 7:17

You stand in the center of God's throne encircled by four living creatures and the elders. You have seven horns and seven eyes, which represent the seven Spirits of God sent out into all the earth.
Revelation 5:6

You are Lord and Savior Jesus Christ.
2 Peter 1:11, 2:20, 3:18

You are Lord of all.
Acts 10:36

You are Lord of the Sabbath.
Matthew 12; Mark 2:28

You are a place of rest.
Isaiah 11:10; Hebrews 4:3; Matthew 11:28-30

You are the Messenger of the covenant.
Malachi 3:1

You are the mediator of a new covenant.
Hebrews 8:6, 9:15, 12:24

You are the only mediator who reconciles God and humanity.
1 Timothy 2:5

You are the guarantor of a better covenant.
Hebrews 7:22

You, the Stone who the builders rejected, have become the Cornerstone.
Psalm 118:22; Matthew 21:42; Mark 12:10; Luke 20:17

Jesus, You are the chief cornerstone of the foundation of apostles and prophets. In You, the members of God's household are being joined together as the whole building, rising to become a holy temple in the Lord, the dwelling place for God.
Ephesians 2:19-21

You are a foundation stone, a tried stone, a precious cornerstone, a sure foundation.
Isaiah 28:16

You are a stone in Zion, a chosen and precious cornerstone.
1 Peter 2:6

You are a sanctuary; but a stone of stumbling and a rock of offense (to the unbeliever).
Isaiah 8:14

You are the True Vine.
John 15:1, 5

You are God's chosen one Who pleases Him. His Spirit is upon You.
Isaiah 42:1

On your head are many crowns, and You have a name written on You that no one knows but yourself.
Revelation 19:12

Jesus, You serve as the Minister in the true heavenly Tabernacle, the authentic sanctuary built by God.
Hebrews 8:2

Jesus, You are dressed in linen clothing, with a belt of pure gold around your waist. Your body looks like a precious gem. Your face flashes like lightning, and your eyes flame like torches. Your arms and legs shine like polished bronze, and your words sound like a vast multitude of people.
Daniel 10:5-6

You are a life-giving Spirit.
1 Corinthians 15:45

You are anointed with the Holy Spirit and power.
Acts 10:38

You are a rose of Sharon, a lily of the valley.
Song of Solomon 2:1

You are the bridegroom.
Matthew 9:15, 25:1; John 3:29; Revelation 21:2, 9

Gracious words proceed out of your mouth.
Luke 4:22

You are the most excellent of men. Your lips have been anointed with grace since God has blessed You forever.
Psalm 45:2

You love righteousness and hate wickedness; therefore God, your God, has anointed You, pouring out the oil of joy on You more than anyone else.
Psalm 45:7; Hebrews 1:9

You are the Prince of Peace.
Isaiah 9:6

You are the consolation of Israel, the redemption of
Jerusalem.
Luke 2:25, 38

You are the seed of Abraham.
Genesis 22:18; Galatians 3:16

You are a star that came forth out of Jacob, and a
scepter that arose from Israel.
Numbers 24:17

You are the root and offspring of David.
Revelation 22:16

You are the righteous branch that sprouted from the
family of David.
Jeremiah 23:5, 33:15

You reign on David's throne and over his kingdom.
Isaiah 9:7

You are the Root of Jesse.
Isaiah 11:10

You are God's servant, the Branch.
Zechariah 3:8

Jesus, You are the last Adam, the second man.
1 Corinthians 15:45, 47

You are the Lord Who sits on the throne, lofty and exalted. The train of your robe fills the temple. Seraphim stand above You, calling out to one another: "Holy, Holy, Holy is the Lord of Hosts. The whole earth is full of His Glory." And the foundations of your thresholds tremble as your temple fills with smoke.
Isaiah 6:1-4

You are the Righteous One.
1 John 2:1; Acts 7:52, 22:14

You are the Holy and Righteous One.
Acts 3:14

You are the Lord Our Righteousness (Yahweh-Tsidkenu).
Jeremiah 23:6

You are the sun of righteousness.
Malachi 4:2

You are the Holy servant.
Acts 4:27

You are a prophet, powerful in action and speech.
Luke 24:19

You are a friend of sinners.
Matthew 11:19; Luke 7:34, 5:30

You are the great Shepherd of the sheep.
Hebrews 13:20

You are the Good Shepherd, the Chief Shepherd.
John 10:11; 1 Peter 5:4

You are the door.
John 10:9

You are the Faithful and True Witness.
Revelation 3:14; 1:5

You are the Apostle.
Hebrews 3:1

You are True.
1 John 5:20; Revelation 3:7

You are the Messiah the Prince.
Daniel 9:25

Jesus, You are worthy to take the scroll from the right hand of the One seated on the throne, and to open its seven seals. The four living creatures, the elders, and millions of angels encircle your throne. Their loud voices are saying, "Worthy is the Lamb Who was slain to receive Power and Riches and Wisdom and Strength and Honor and Glory and Blessing!" Every created thing in heaven and on earth, under the earth, and in the sea, and all that is in them, says, "To Him Who sits on the throne, and to the Lamb, be Praise, Honor, Glory, and Power forever and ever!"
Revelation 5:7, 9-13

You are the sinless spotless Lamb.
1 Peter 1:19

You are the Lamb of God Who takes away the sin of the world.
John 1:29, 36

You are He Who was dead and Who lives.
Revelation 1:18

You are the Priest that offered for all time one sacrifice for sins, then You sat down at the right hand of God.
Hebrews 10:12

You are an anchor.
Hebrews 6:19

You are the Good Teacher.
Luke 18:18; Mark 10:17

You are the Rabbi.
John 1:38, 49, 3:2, 26, 6:25 and many more.

You are Master.
Luke 5:5, 17:13

You are a Priest forever in the priestly order of Melchizedek.
Psalm 110:4; Hebrews 7:17

You are the Great High Priest over the house of God.
Hebrews 4:14, 10:21

You are a merciful and faithful High Priest in service to God.
Hebrews 2:17

You are the Head of the Church, which is your body.
Colossians 1:18

You are faithful as the Son over God's house.
Hebrews 3:6

You are Ruler over Israel.
Micah 5:2

You are Ruler of the kings of the earth.
Revelation 1:5

You are King of kings and Lord of lords.
1 Timothy 6:15; Revelation 17:14, 19:16

You are the Savior of the world.
1 John 4:14; John 4:42

You are the Author of eternal salvation.
Hebrews 2:10, 5:9

You are the Deliverer.
Romans 11:26

You are the Resurrection and the Life.
John 11:25

You are Judge of the living and the dead.
Acts 10:42; 2 Timothy 4:1

You, Jesus, are the One appointed by God to judge the
world with justice on the appointed day.
Acts 17:31; John 5:22

You came with the clouds of heaven; One like a human being, and You came up to the Ancient of Days and were presented before Him. And You were given Dominion, Glory, and a Kingdom, that all the peoples, nations and men of every language should serve You. Your dominion is an everlasting dominion that will never end, and your Kingdom will never be destroyed.
Daniel 7:13-14

You are Alive forevermore!
Revelation 1:18

You hold the keys of death and Hades.
Revelation 1:18

At your name, every knee bows in heaven and on earth and under the earth, and every tongue declares that You are Lord, to the glory of God the Father.
Philippians 2:10-11

You are the Alpha and the Omega, the First and the Last, the Beginning and the End.
Revelation 22:13

Your words will never pass away, even when heaven and earth pass away.
Matthew 24:35; Mark 13:31; Luke 21:33

Your throne will last forever and ever.
Psalm 45:6; Hebrews 1:8

6

WHAT JESUS DOES

You hold all creation together.
Colossians 1:17

You came into the world You created.
John 1:9-10

You sustain everything by your powerful Word.
Hebrews 1:3

You came from heaven.
John 6:38

You are the Word Who became human and made your dwelling among us.
John 1:14

You knew that the Father had given You authority over everything, and that You came from Him and would return to Him.
John 13:3

You did not consider equality with God something to be used to your own advantage.
Philippians 2:6

You took the humble position of a servant, born as a human being.
Philippians 2:7

You were conceived in the womb of a virgin.
Isaiah 7:14; Luke 1:31; Matthew 1:23

You have come forth from Bethlehem, among the clans of Judah, as prophesied, destined to rule in Israel and shepherd God's people.
Micah 5:2; Matthew 2:6

You were born and came into the world to testify to the truth.
John 18:37

You were born under the law to redeem those who are under the law.
Galatians 4:4-5

You did nothing on your own. You only did what You saw the Father doing. Whatever the Father did, You did likewise.
John 5:19

The words You spoke were not on your own initiative; rather, it was the Father living in You performing His works.
John 14:10

You have the words of eternal life, and your words are Spirit and Life.
John 6:63, 68

You do not judge by outward appearances, but judge with righteous judgment.
John 7:24

You do not judge by appearance or make
decisions based on hearsay.
Isaiah 11:3

You taught in the synagogues, proclaiming the gospel
of the kingdom, and healed every kind of disease and
sickness among the people.
Matthew 4:23

You are anointed with the Holy Spirit and with
power. Everywhere You go, You do good and heal all
who are oppressed by the devil, for God is with you.
Acts 10:38

You drive out evil spirits with a word and heal all who
are sick.
Matthew 8:16

Jesus, You are the same yesterday, today and forever.
Hebrews 13:8

You bring good news to the poor, proclaim freedom
for the prisoners, heal the brokenhearted, and
declare the year of the Lord's favor.
Luke 4:18

You emphasize, "Love the Lord your God with all
your heart and with all your soul and with all your
mind. This is the first and greatest commandment.
And the second is like it: Love your neighbor as
yourself."
Matthew 22:37-39

You raised Lazarus from the tomb after being dead
for four days.
John 11:38-45

When You were transfigured before Peter, James, and John on a high mountain, your face shone like the sun, and your clothes became dazzling white. When Moses and Elijah appeared in glory, You conversed with them about your departure, which You were to accomplish in Jerusalem. Then a bright cloud enveloped them, and a voice from the cloud declared, "This is My beloved Son, in whom I am well pleased. Listen to Him!" Upon hearing this, the disciples fell facedown.

Matthew 17:1-6; Mark 9:2-7; Luke 9:28-32

While You were in Bethany, at the home of Simon, a woman approached You with an alabaster jar of expensive perfume. She poured it on your head as You were reclining at the table. You commended her act, saying that she has done a beautiful thing by anointing your body in preparation for burial. You said, "Truly, wherever this Gospel is preached in all the world, what she has done will also be told in memory of her."

Mark 14:3-9; Matthew 26:6-13

Knowing that a band of soldiers, officers, chief priests, and Pharisees were coming to arrest You, You asked them, "Whom are you seeking?" They replied, "Jesus of Nazareth." You answered, "I Am He." Suddenly they drew back and fell to the ground. Following this, You were arrested and bound.

John 18:4-8, 12

When You stood before the governor, accused
by the chief priests and elders, You remained
silent. Pilate asked, "Do You not hear how many
things they testify against You?" But You chose
not to answer him.
Matthew 27:11-14

You were oppressed and afflicted, yet You did
not open your mouth; You were led like a lamb
to the slaughter.
Isaiah 53:7

You know and understand pain and grief.
Isaiah 53:3; Luke 22:44; Mark 15:22; Hebrews 5:7

You humbled yourself by becoming obedient to
the point of death.
Philippians 2:8

You suffered once for sins, the righteous for
the unrighteous, to bring mankind to God.
1 Peter 3:18

You endured such hostility from sinners.
Hebrews 12:3

You gave yourself as a ransom for all.
1 Timothy 2:6

You were faithful to God Who appointed You.
Hebrews 3:2

You learned obedience through what You
suffered. And being made perfect, You became
the source of eternal salvation to all who obey
You.
Hebrews 5:8-9

You, Jesus, the promised Messiah, fulfilled the
prophecy, atoning for the people's guilt and
bringing forth everlasting righteousness.
Daniel 9:24-25

By your one sacrifice, You have perfected forever
those who are being made holy.
Hebrews 10:14

You were slain and with your blood You purchased
for God those from every tribe, language, people,
and nation.
Revelation 5:9

After being on the cross for three hours, the sun became
obscured, and for the next three hours, darkness covered the
land. Then You cried out, "Father, into your hands I commit
My Spirit" and proclaimed, "It is finished."
Luke 23:44-46; John 19:30

At that moment, the curtain in the temple was torn
in two from top to bottom. There was an earthquake,
and rocks were split open. The centurion and
soldiers exclaimed, "Truly this was the Son of God!"
Matthew 27:51, 54

At the same time, tombs broke open, and many godly men and women who had died were awakened, but were not allowed to leave their tombs just yet.
Matthew 27:52

Your body was placed in a tomb cut out of rock and sealed with a large circular stone. An official Roman seal was set upon it, and guards were posted to secure it.
Matthew 27:60, 65-66

After three days, an angel whose appearance was like lightning and who was dressed in white descended from heaven, causing a violent earthquake. Then, the angel rolled away the stone and sat on it. The guards were so terrified of him that they shook and became petrified!
Matthew 28:2-4

Shortly after, Mary Magdalene arrived, weeping, and bent down to look into the opened, empty tomb. There inside, she saw two angels in white sitting where your body had been—one at the head and the other at the feet. Suddenly, she heard You call her name. Turning around, she exclaimed, "Rabboni!" You instructed her to go and tell your brothers that You are ascending to your Father and their Father, to your God and their God.
John 20:11-12, 14, 16-17

Those who had been restricted from leaving their tombs at the time of your death were now freed, for it was necessary for You to be the first to rise permanently from the dead. They then entered the walled, gated city of Jerusalem, about half a mile away, and were seen by many.
Matthew 27:53; 1 Corinthians 15:20-23

You disarmed the powers and authorities, making a public spectacle of them, triumphing over them by your cross.
Colossians 2:15

You broke the power of death and illuminated the way to life and immortality.
2 Timothy 1:10

During the forty days following your resurrection, You appeared to the apostles numerous times discussing the Kingdom of God providing them with substantial evidence of your resurrection.
Acts 1:3

On one occasion while dining with them, You commanded them not to depart from Jerusalem until the Father sends the Holy Spirit to baptize them.
Acts 1:4-5

You also told your disciples that when the Holy Spirit comes upon them, they would receive power and would be your witnesses even to the ends of the earth.
Act 1:8

Again, You appeared to your disciples and said, "All authority in heaven and on earth has been given to Me."
Matthew 28:18

Your final instructions were to go into all the world and preach the Gospel, making disciples of all nations, baptizing them, and teaching them to obey your commands. You affirmed that these signs will accompany those who believe: They will cast out demons in your name, speak in new tongues, have protection from harmful substances, and lay their hands on the sick to see them recover.
Matthew 28:19-20; Mark 16:15-18

After commissioning them, and as they were watching, You were lifted up, and a cloud concealed You from their sight.
Acts 1:9; Luke 24:51

When You ascended to the heights, You led a crowd of captives and gave gifts to people.
Ephesians 4:8, 10; Psalm 68:18

With the clouds of heaven, You were led into God's presence. You were given authority, glory, and sovereign power.
Daniel 7:13-14; 1 Corinthians 15:24

Ten days later, the one hundred and twenty were filled with the Holy Spirit. From that point on, the Gospel is spoken boldly, and manifestations of healings and miracles continue to be performed.
The Book of Acts and beyond.

You make all things new.
Revelation 21:5

You descended to the lower parts of the earth and then ascended above all the heavens, in order to fill all things.
Ephesians 4:9-10

You will come again, not to bear sin, but to bring salvation to all who are eagerly awaiting your return.
Hebrews 9:28

You are to remain in heaven until the time when all things are finally restored, fulfilling God's ancient promise through His holy prophets.
Acts 3:21

Jesus, from the span of time between your resurrection and your second coming, God gave You authority over all things except over God himself.
1 Corinthians 15:23-28

Jesus, You must reign (in heaven) until You have placed all your enemies under your feet. The last enemy to be destroyed is death.
1 Corinthians 15:25

You will return just as You were seen ascending into heaven.
Acts 1:11

Every eye will see you.
Revelation 1:7

At that time, Heaven will open, and You, Jesus, the Faithful and True, will come on clouds in great glory, riding a white horse. The armies of heaven will follow you. Your robe is dipped in blood, and You are named the Word of God. 'KING OF KINGS AND LORD OF LORDS' is written on your robe and thigh!
Revelation 19:11, 13, 16

Then in one moment, in the twinkle of an eye, the believers who have passed away and those still alive will be changed and will join You in the clouds!
1 Corinthians 15:52; 1 Thessalonians 4:16-17

After the times of trial, You will return in all your glory, seated on your glorious throne. Every deed and hidden thing, whether good or evil, will be uncovered, revealing the hearts of all. You will separate people like a shepherd divides sheep from goats. The sheep will stand on your right and the goats on your left. To those on your right, You will say, "Come, you who are blessed by My Father, inherit the kingdom prepared for you since the world began." To those on your left, You will say, "Depart from Me, you who are cursed, into the eternal fire prepared for the devil and his angels." This fate also awaits the beast, the false prophet, and the kings of the earth who waged war against You and deceived many. With the power of your Word, like a sword proceeding from your mouth, You will vanquish all who worshiped the beast's image.
Matthew 25:31; Hebrews 4:13; Ecclesiastes 12:14; Matthew 25:32-34, 41, 46; Revelation 14:9-11, 19:19-20, 20:10-12, 14-15

After all things are subjected to the authority of your Father, You, Jesus, will willingly subject yourself under God's authority, so that God may be all in all.
1 Corinthians 15:28

You have overcome the world.
John 16:33

All nations and peoples of every language worship You. Your dominion is an everlasting dominion that will not pass away, and your Kingdom will never be destroyed.
Daniel 7:14

You build your church, and all the powers of hell will not conquer it.
Matthew 16:18

You are the Amen.
Revelation 3:14

You are coming soon.
Revelation 22:20

7

WHO JESUS IS TO ME

You are my beginning.
Colossians 1:18

You chose me.
John 15:16

You are my Savior.
Titus 2:13-14; Acts 4:12

You are my spiritual food, my bread from heaven, my bread of life.
1 Corinthians 10:3-5; John 6:32-33, 48, 50-51

You are Living Bread offered for me. You promise eternal life if I partake of You.
John 6:51

You are my spiritual rock from which spiritual drinking water gushes out.
1 Corinthians 10:4; Numbers 20:8, 11

You are my Prince.
Isaiah 9:6

You are my King.
Revelation 19:16

You are my bridegroom.
John 3:29; Matthew 9:15, 25:1-13; Revelation 21:2, 9

You love me.
Romans 8:38; Ephesians 2:4; John 3:16

Your love for me is as strong as death.
Song of Solomon 8:6; Romans 5:8

Jesus, You, and the Father have made your home in me because I love You and keep your word.
John 14:23-24; 1 John 2:24

You live in me.
Galatians 2:20

You live in me because I acknowledge You as the Son of God.
1 John 4:15, 2:23

You remain in me as I remain in You, as a branch remains in the Vine.
John 15:4-5

By this I know that You abide in me, by the Spirit You have given me.
1 John 3:24, 4:13

God predestined me to become like You, Jesus.
Romans 8:29

Your desire for me is to constantly bear your likeness.
1 Corinthians 15:48-49

Jesus, as You are, so am I in this world.
1 John 4:15, 17; 1 Corinthians 15:48

Your joy is in me, and your joy is made complete as I
remain in You and keep your command to love others.
John 15:10-12

You are the atoning sacrifice for my sins.
1 John 2:2, 4:10; Romans 3:25

God made You—Jesus—who had no sin—to be sin for
me; so that in You, I become the righteousness of God
(having God's judicial approval).
2 Corinthians 5:21

You are my righteousness.
Jeremiah 23:6; Philippians 3:9; 2 Corinthians 5:21

Jesus, before faith, I was under the law's custody, as
my guardian. Now, in You, I am free—a child of God
through faith, no longer captive.
Galatians 3:23-26

Jesus, through God's grace, You and I have been raised
up and are now positioned with God in the heavenly
realms.
Ephesians 2:6

Through You I have gained access by faith into this
grace in which I now stand.
Romans 5:2

The word of faith I proclaim is very close at hand; it is on my lips and in my heart. I am saved because I openly declare that You are Lord, and I believe in my heart that God raised You from the dead.
Romans 10:8-9

From your abundance, Jesus, I receive grace upon grace (favor, kindness, gifts, blessings).
John 1:16

You are my Restorer.
Acts 3:21; 1 Peter 5:10

You are my Healer.
Matthew 4:23

You have become for me wisdom from God: my righteousness, my holiness, and my redemption.
1 Corinthians 1:30

Jesus, when I ask, seek, and knock, I receive, find, and see doors open, for my Father in heaven imparts good gifts to those who request of Him.
Matthew 7:7-11

You say that I am blessed for being merciful, and in turn, I will be shown mercy.
Matthew 5:7

You call me to become like You in your death, participate in your sufferings, and know the power of your resurrection.
Philippians 3:10

Since I am an heir of God and a co-heir with You, I know that I will share in your sufferings that I may also share in your glory.
Romans 8:17

You know me.
John 2:24, 10:14, 10:27

You are near to me when I call on You, when I call out to You in truth.
Psalm 145:18

You fellowship with me.
1 Corinthians 1:9; Revelation 3:20

You know my thoughts.
Matthew 9:4; Luke 9:47

You invite me to come to You when I am weary and when I am carrying heavy burdens. You want me to take your yoke upon myself and learn from You and find rest for my soul.
Matthew 11:28-29

Jesus, your power rests on me when I gladly boast about my weaknesses, for your power is made perfect in my weakness.
2 Corinthians 12:9

You are my Sanctifier.
John 17:19

Jesus, You say that I am blessed when people insult me, persecute me, and falsely say all sorts of evil things against me because I follow You. You encourage me to find joy in these trials, for a great reward awaits me in heaven.
Matthew 5:11-12; Luke 6:22-23

You are like a refiner's fire…refining and purifying me like gold and silver.
Malachi 3:2-3

Just as gold is refined through purifying fire, You use my temporary trials to strengthen and purify my faith, resulting in Praise, Glory, and Honor on the day of your return. Therefore, I rejoice!
1 Peter 1:6-8

You want me to rejoice in my sufferings because it produces perseverance, character, and hope.
Romans 5:3

These trials unite me with You in your suffering, providing me with the wonderful joy of witnessing your glory when it is revealed to all the world.
1 Peter 4:13

It is a blessing when I am insulted for bearing your name, for the Spirit of Glory and of God rests on me. I am not ashamed of being a Christian.
1 Peter 4:14, 16

This treasure I have inside of me (me being a mere clay jar) is proof that this surpassingly great power is not from me, but from You, Jesus!
2 Corinthians 4:7

You are Christ in me, giving me the hope of glory.
Colossians 1:27

Your Father draws me to You because I listen and learn from Him.
John 6:44-45

Jesus, as the only One Who has ever seen God and being God yourself, so close to the Father's heart, You reveal Him to me.
John 1:18; 6:46

You are where two or three gather in your name.
Matthew 18:20

You are my judge.
2 Timothy 4:1; John 5:22; 1 Corinthians 4:4-5

I refrain from passing judgment upon myself.
1 Corinthians 4:3-4

You are my Advocate Who pleads my case before my Father when I sin.
1 John 2:1

You are at the right hand of God interceding for me.
Romans 8:34

You no longer call me servant because a master does not confide in his servants. You call me your friend, for everything You have learned from the Father You have made known to me as your command.
John 15:15

Jesus, You say that if I do your Father's will that I am your brother/sister, mother/father.
Matthew 12:46-50

You call me to love my enemies and pray for those who persecute me, that I may be a son/daughter of my Father in heaven.
Matthew 5:44-45

Both You, the One Who sanctifies, and we who are being sanctified, are of the same family with one Father. Therefore You, Jesus, are not ashamed to call us your brothers and sisters.
Hebrews 2:11

God sent You to be the oldest son (firstborn) of many brothers and sisters and He preplanned me to be one of them.
Romans 8:29

Jesus, You said that if You, as the head of the household, have been called Beelzebul, then as part of your household, I might also face even worse names.
Matthew 10:25

In You, I have peace.
John 16:33; John 14:27

You are my Sabbath rest.
Hebrews 4:3, 6, 9-10

You are my Messiah.
Matthew 16:16; John 20:31

You are my Teacher and Lord.
John 13:13-14

You are my Instructor.
Matthew 23:10

You are my Shepherd.
Hebrews 13:20; 1 Peter 2:25

You are the Overseer of my soul.
1 Peter 2:25

You are the Author of my faith.
Hebrews 12:2

You are the Perfector of my faith.
Hebrews 12:2

In You is life, and your life is my light.
John 1:4

You will not abandon me.
John 14:18

You are with me always, even to the end of the age.
Matthew 28:20

You invite me to your wedding feast.
Revelation 19:9; Luke 14:15; Matthew 22:2

You will be glorified in me on the day You come.
2 Thessalonians 1:10

8

WHAT JESUS DOES FOR ME

By your blood You purchased me for God to become a
priest, and You made us to be a kingdom to serve God
and reign on the earth.
Revelation 5:9-10

You gave yourself up for me.
Galatians 2:20

You have given me the right and power to be born
again; to become a child of God because I believe in
You, receive You, and put my trust in your Name.
John 1:12-13

Jesus, You have given me access by faith into this grace
in which I stand. And I rejoice in the hope of sharing in
the glory of God.
Romans 5:2

You have opened a new and living way through the
curtain, which is your body. Because of this, I can
confidently enter the Most Holy Place by your blood,
my sins forgiven, with no need for any more sacrifices.
Hebrews 10:17-22

You are my door. I enter through You and am saved.
John 10:9

Jesus, it is on my behalf that You have entered the inner sanctuary behind the curtain, providing me with this hope, like an anchor for my soul, firm and secure. You are my priest forever in the order of Melchizedek.
Hebrews 6:19-20

You are my forerunner having entered the inner sanctuary on my behalf.
Hebrews 6:15-20

You canceled the record of the charges that stood against me. You took it away nailing it to your cross.
Colossians 2:14

You invite me to come boldly to God's throne of grace.
Hebrews 4:16

God lavished upon me, according to the riches of His grace, the forgiveness of my sins through your blood, Jesus.
Ephesians 1:7-8

You ended the system of laws with its commandments and regulations.
Ephesians 2:15

Jesus, You remain faithful to me even when I am unfaithful to You, for You cannot deny Who You are within me.
2 Timothy 2:13

It is for freedom You have set me free.
Galatians 5:1

Jesus, You offer moments of refreshment when my heart turns to repentance, resulting in the cleansing of my sins.
Acts 3:19-20

You have called me out of darkness into your marvelous light.
1 Peter 2:9

You saved me by grace through faith, a gift of God not of my own doing or from my own works.
Ephesians 2:8-9

You are the dawn from heaven breaking over me guiding me down the path of peace.
Luke 1:78-79

Jesus, You are transforming me into your image with ever-increasing glory. As I turn to You, the veil is removed, and with unveiled face, I reflect your glory.
2 Corinthians 3:16, 18

You confirmed your covenant with me by pouring out your own blood for me.
Luke 22:20; Hebrews 7:22

You purged my sins and sat down at the right hand of the Majesty on High.
Hebrews 1:3

It is through your strength alone that I can do all things.
Philippians 4:13

Jesus, I understand that when I pray, I must begin by forgiving anyone I hold grudges against, so that my Father in heaven will also forgive my sins.
Mark 11:25; Matthew 6:14; Luke 11:4

You said that whatever I ask You for in prayer, and if I believe I have received it, it will be mine.
Mark 11:24; Matthew 21:22; John 16:23

Jesus, I believe that I will receive from God whatever I ask because I believe in You, love others, and do what pleases God.
1 John 3:22-23

Again, You said that if two of us here on earth agree about anything we ask for, it will be done for us by our Father in heaven.
Matthew 18:19

Jesus, You said that if I command this mountain, 'Go and throw yourself into the sea,' and if I do not doubt in my heart but believe that it will happen, it will be done for me.
Mark 11:23

According to my faith, You heal me, just as You did for the many people whom You healed due to their faith.
Matthew 8:13, 9:22, 28-29, 15:28; Mark 5:34, 10:52, and 17 more

Through You I have been justified through faith and have peace with God.
Romans 5:1

Jesus, You fulfilled Isaiah's prophecy by healing the centurion's paralyzed servant, Peter's mother-in-law who was sick with fever, and all who were sick. This was to fulfill what was spoken through the prophet Isaiah: 'He himself took our infirmities and carried away our diseases.'
Matthew 8:6-7, 13-15, 17

Lord, You bore my sufferings, were pierced for my rebellion, crushed for my guilt, and beaten to make me whole. You took my sickness upon yourself, and by your stripes (wounds from being whipped), I am healed.
Isaiah 53:4-5

(Matthew 8:17 NASB says, "He himself took our infirmities and carried away our diseases." This closely matches Isaiah 53:4-5 NRSV, which says, "Surely He has borne our infirmities and carried our diseases… and by his bruises we are healed.")

You bore my sins in your body on the cross… and by your wounds, I am (physically) healed.
1 Peter 2:24
(Healed, in Greek, is 'iaomai' (ἰάομαι), which in this passage pertains predominantly to physical healing. 'Iaomai' is used an additional 23 times to describe the physical healings performed by Jesus and the apostles.)

You cast out demons and give your disciples the authority to do the same.
Matthew 8:16, 10:8; Mark 5:13; Luke 9:1; Acts 16:18; Luke 10:17

You freed me from being a slave to the fear of death when You broke the power of the devil who had the power of death.
Hebrews 2:14-15

You have given me authority, so that I can walk on snakes and scorpions and overcome all the power of the enemy, and nothing will hurt me.
Luke 10:19; Psalm 91:13-14

You exist eternally to intercede on my behalf.
Hebrews 7:25

You were handed over to die for my sins, and You were raised to life to make me right with God.
Romans 4:25

You redeemed me from the curse of the law by becoming a curse for me.
Galatians 3:13

You willingly gave your life to save me from sin, in accordance with my Father's divine plan, rescuing me from the grip of this present evil age.
Galatians 1:4

Through You, the law of the Spirit of life has set me free from the law of sin and death.
Romans 8:2

Jesus, You sympathize with my weaknesses, having faced the same temptations that confront me, yet you did so without sin.
Hebrews 4:15

You suffered when You were tempted, which enables You to aid me when I face temptation.
Hebrews 2:18

You do not allow the temptation to be more than I can stand. When I am tempted You are faithful to provide a way out so that I can endure it.
1 Corinthians 10:13

You are deeply moved in your Spirit and greatly troubled when there is sorrow caused by death, and You weep with empathy with those who grieve.
John 11:33-35

You comfort me when I mourn.
Matthew 5:4

You, the Chief Cornerstone, have united me with other members of God's household, and we are together building on your foundation, along with the apostles and prophets. The building is rising, becoming God's dwelling place, a Holy Temple in the Lord.
Ephesians 2:19-22

You want me to meet with other members of God's household to spur one another on to love and good deeds, to encourage one another, especially now that the day of your return is drawing near.
Hebrews 10:24-25

Jesus, as I am rooted and grounded in your love, You will give me, together with all believers, the power to comprehend the length, width, height, and depth of your love—that surpasses knowledge, so that I may be filled with the fullness of God.
Ephesians 3:16-19

You baptize me with your Holy Spirit and with fire.
Luke 3:16

Jesus, You said that because I believe in You, I also will
do the works that You did. You also said that I will do
even greater works than You, so that the Father may be
glorified in You.
John 14:12-13

You are the vine; I am a branch. If I remain in You and
You in me, I will bear much fruit; apart from You, I can
do nothing.
John 15:5

Jesus, You chose me and appointed me to live in
partnership with You, producing fruit (works) that last
and reflect our union—works that You promise to
honor by granting whatever I ask in your name.
John 15:16

You call me to produce fruit consistent with
repentance.
Matthew 3:8

You deliver me from the wrath to come.
1 Thessalonians 1:10

Jesus, You emphasized that the righteous and the
wicked will coexist until the time of final judgment
when You will separate them.
Matthew 13:24-30

You are able to keep me from stumbling and to present me before your glorious presence without fault and with great joy.
Jude 2:4

You will acknowledge me before the angels of God if I acknowledge you publicly here on earth.
Luke 12:8

You will lead me to springs of living water. You invite me to freely drink from the water of life.
Revelation 7:17, 22:17

Jesus, You are coming soon, bringing your reward with You, to repay me according to my deeds.
Revelation 22:12; Isaiah 62:11; Matthew 25:14-31

Holding fast, keeping your word, and persevering so that no one will take my crown, You will keep me from the hour of testing about to come upon the world, to test those who dwell on the earth.
Revelation 3:10-11

When You return, You will call me into the clouds to meet You in the air, where I will be with You always.
1 Thessalonians 4:17; Matthew 24:31

When I overcome, You will make me a pillar in the temple of God, and inscribe upon me your name, your new name, and the name of the City of God (the new Jerusalem descending from heaven).
Revelation 3:12

When I overcome, You grant me the right to eat from the tree of life in the Paradise of God.
Revelation 2:7

You promise me access to the hidden manna in heaven. Additionally, You will give me a white stone, upon which a new name will be engraved, known only to You and me.
Revelation 2:17

Jesus, You prepare a place for me. You will come back and take me to be with You so that I may be where You are.
John 14:3

9

WHO HOLY SPIRIT IS

You are the Eternal Spirit.
Hebrews 9:14

You were sent from heaven.
1 Peter 1:12

You are the breath of God.
Genesis 2:7; John 20:22; Ezekial 37:9-10 and many more.

You are the wind of God.
John 3:6-8; Acts 2:2

You are Living Water. Whoever drinks You will never thirst again.
John 4:10, 13; Zechariah 14:8

You are the water Jesus gives that becomes a fountain springing up to eternal life.
John 4:14

You are the gift from God.
Acts 10:45, 11:17

You are the gift to be received by those who repent and accept Jesus Christ for the forgiveness of their sins.
Acts 2:38

You are the gift the Father promised to send.
Acts 1:4, 2:39; Luke 24:49

You are given to those who obey God.
Acts 5:32

You, the Spirit, are given to those who ask of the Father.
Luke 11:13

You are the advocate, the Spirit of truth sent by Jesus, and You proceed from the Father.
John 15:26

You live within a person's inner being. (their inward part, deep within them).
Ephesians 3:16; 1 John 4:13

You are the power to be God's witnesses.
Acts 1:8

You are the Spirit of God.
Genesis 1:2; 1 Corinthians 2:11; Romans 8:9 and many more.

You are the Spirit of Christ.
1 Peter 1:11; Romans 8:9; Philippians 1:19

You are the Spirit of Jesus.
Galatians 4:6; Acts 16:7

You are the Spirit God placed upon Jesus.
Isaiah 42:1; Matthew 12:18

You are the life in Jesus' words.
John 6:63

You are the Spirit of Life.
Romans 8:2

You are the Spirit of Glory.
1 Peter 4:14

You are the Spirit of Holiness.
Romans 1:4

You are the Spirit of Adoption.
Romans 8:15

You are the Spirit of Counsel.
Isaiah 11:2

You are the Counselor.
John 14:26

You are the Spirit of Truth.
John 14:17, 15:26, 16:13; 1 John 4:6

Holy Spirit, You are the One that God anointed Jesus
with to heal all who were oppressed by the devil.
Acts 10:38

You are the Spirit of the Lord Who anointed Jesus to do
His works.
Isaiah 61:1; Luke 4:18

Your revealed truth is the witness of Jesus.
Revelation 19:10

You are required for someone to say, "Jesus is Lord."
1 Corinthians 12:3

You are a spirit of grace and supplication.
Zechariah 12:10

You, Holy Spirit, are the unity in the Body of Christ.
Ephesians 4:3-5

You are the breath of God that gives understanding.
Job 32:8

You are a guide.
John 16:13

You are a teacher.
John 14:26

You, the Spirit of truth, are the discerning factor in recognizing those who are of God and listen to us, and those who are not of God and do not listen to us.
1 John 4:6

You are the helper.
John 14:26

Holy Spirit, Your sword is the Word of God.
Ephesians 6:17

The baptism of You is accompanied with fire.
Matthew 3:11; Luke 3:16; Acts 2:3-4

Your sound was like a mighty rushing wind.
Acts 2:2

The place where You came was shaken.
Acts 4:31

The people You fill become bold.
Acts 4:13, 31

Where You are, there is freedom.
2 Corinthians 3:17

Holy Spirit, You are greater than the spirit who is in the world (the devil).
1 John 4:4

You, Holy Spirit, are a witness that God raised Jesus from the dead and exalted Him as Savior to grant repentance and forgiveness of sins.
Acts 5:31-32

You are the Spirit of the Lord, the Spirit of Wisdom and of Understanding, the Spirit of Counsel, the Spirit of Might, the Spirit of Knowledge, and Fear of the Lord.
Isaiah 11:2
(Traditionally, the 7 Lamps of Fire before God's Throne in Revelation 4:5 symbolize these attributes of the Holy Spirit.)

It is through You, the one Spirit, the same Spirit, that the variety of manifestations are given for the good of all: the message of wisdom, the message of knowledge, faith, gifts of healing, miraculous results, prophecy, distinguishing between spirits, speaking in tongues, and interpretation of tongues.
1 Corinthians 12:4-10

10

WHAT HOLY SPIRIT DOES

When the earth was formless and empty, and darkness covered the deep waters, your presence, O Spirit of God, was hovering over the surface of the waters. Then God said, "Let there be light," and there was light.
Genesis 1:2-3

By You, God adorned the heavens.
Job 26:13

You, as the breath of God's mouth, by the word of the Lord, were instrumental in creating the heavens and the stars.
Psalm 33:6

God breathed You, the breath of life, into Adam's nostrils and he became a living being.
Genesis 2:7

You give Life.
John 6:63

You were the cool of the day (the wind, the Spirit) as the Lord God walked in the Garden of Eden.
Genesis 3:8

You were the wind over the earth Who subsided the waters in Noah's day.
Genesis 8:1

Holy Spirit, it was your presence that dwelt among the Israelites when God, through Moses, sent His glorious arm of power to part the Red Sea before them.
Isaiah 63:11-12

You, the Spirit, were within the Israelites that caused them to walk in God's statutes and ordinances.
Ezekiel 36:27

Ezekiel prophesied that God would breathe You into the Israelites (into their hopeless state like dry bones) and they would come to life and be brought back to their homeland Israel.
Ezekiel 37:10, 14

God said to Moses, "I will take some of the Spirit that is on you and put that Spirit on the seventy elders of Israel at the tent of meeting to help you bear the burden of the people, so that you do not have to bear it by yourself."
Numbers 11:17

Then You, the Spirit, at the tent of meeting, rested on, and caused Moses and the seventy elders to prophesy. At the same time, You even rested on two of the elders who stayed in the camp, who also prophesied. And Moses said to Joshua, "I wish that all the Lord's people were prophets and that the Lord would put His Spirit on all of them!"
Numbers 11:25-29

Prophets speak from God as they are being carried along by You, the Holy Spirit.
2 Peter 1:21

You, the Spirit, filled Bezalel with skill, ability, and knowledge so that he along with Oholiab could construct the Ark of the Covenant, and other elements of the tabernacle, including the Mercy Seat. They also used their skills, and taught others, in woodworking, metalworking, designing, engraving, weaving, and artistic designs of every craft for the tabernacle.
Exodus 31:1-6, 35:30-35

When Balaam looked out and saw Israel encamped tribe by tribe, You, the Spirit of God, came upon him and he prophesied a blessing over Israel.
Numbers 24:2-3

It was You, Holy Spirit, Who grieved when the children of Israel rebelled.
Isaiah 63:10

Moses was instructed by God to lay hands on, give authority, and commission Joshua, a man who had You in him.
Numbers 27:18-19

You gave the Israelites rest on every side. God did this to make for himself a glorious name.
Isaiah 63:14

Holy Spirit, as God spoke to Samuel, it was revealed that after anointing Saul as king over Israel, You, the Spirit of the Lord, would come powerfully upon him, enabling him to prophesy alongside other prophets. When Saul encountered the group in Gibeah, You, the Spirit of God, rushed upon him, and he uttered prophesies in unison with these prophets. All who had known Saul previously proclaimed, "What has happened to the son of Kish?" And it became a proverb: "Is Saul also among the prophets?"
1 Samuel 10:1, 5-7, 10-13

You, Holy Spirit, departed from King Saul after Samuel took the horn of oil and anointed David as king. You, the Spirit, came powerfully upon David from that day forward.
1 Samuel 16:13-14

You, the Spirit of the Lord, spoke through the Psalmist David. Your word was on his tongue.
2 Samuel 23:2-3

You spoke through King David when he asked, "Why do the nations rage, and the peoples plot in vain?"
Acts 4:25; Psalm 2:1

You, Holy Spirit, inspired David to speak about his Lord, referring to the Lord Jesus, when he said, 'The Lord said to my Lord, "Sit at My right hand until I make your enemies your footstool."'
Matthew 22:43-44; Mark 12:36-37; Psalm 110:1

Elisha picked up the cloak that had fallen when Elijah was taken up into heaven in a whirlwind. But when the fifty sons of the prophets saw this miraculous event, they thought You, Holy Spirit, had picked up Elijah and placed him on a mountain or in a valley, not acknowledging he had been taken to heaven.
2 Kings 2:11, 13, 15-16

The angel told Zerubbabel that the rebuilding of God's temple would not be by might nor by power, but by You, God's Spirit.
Zechariah 4:6

You, the Spirit, lifted Ezekiel and carried him up in a vision from God. In the vision, he beheld the glory of the Lord in His dwelling place. Then You, the Spirit, came into him, raised him to his feet, and gave him instructions.
Ezekiel 3:12, 24

Holy Spirit, the Lord used You to awaken King Cyrus' spirit to assist in the rebuilding of the Lord's house in Jerusalem. Furthermore, the spirits of the people were stirred to return to Jerusalem to prepare for the work.
Ezra 1:1-2, 5

You, the Spirit of Christ, were within the prophets of old who searched intently and foretold of the grace to come, endeavoring to determine the time and setting, predicting the sufferings of Christ and the glories to follow.
1 Peter 1:10-12

The angel Gabriel foretold Zechariah that, despite Elizabeth's barrenness, she would give birth to John, who would be filled with You, the Holy Spirit.
Luke 1:13-15

Zechariah, himself filled with You, prophesied that his son John would be a prophet preparing the way for the coming dawn (the Messiah). As the child grew, he became strong in spirit.
Luke 1:67, 76, 78-80

John the Baptist was a man with You, the Spirit, and power of Elijah.
Luke 1:17

You, the Holy Spirit, came upon Mary, and the power of the Most High overshadowed her, resulting in the Holy One being born, Who was named the Son of God.
Luke 1:35

An angel of the Lord appeared to Joseph in a dream, revealing that the One in Mary's womb was conceived by You, the Holy Spirit.
Matthew 1:20

You, Holy Spirit, filled Elizabeth the moment she heard Mary's greeting. Elizabeth's own baby leaped for joy in her womb, and she prophesied to Mary in a loud voice saying, "Blessed is the fruit of your womb . . . !"
Luke 1:41-42

O Holy Spirit, it was by your guidance that Simeon was led to the temple in Jerusalem on the day Mary and Joseph presented baby Jesus. You had revealed to him that he would not pass away before beholding the Lord's Messiah. With your presence upon him, Simeon embraced the child and praised God, saying, "Lord, now let your servant die in peace, as You have promised. I have seen your salvation, which You have prepared for all people. He is a light to reveal God to the nations, and He is the glory of your people Israel!"
Luke 2:25-32

John the Baptist spoke of You, Holy Spirit, as the One who would baptize with yourself and with fire.
Luke 3:16; Matthew 3:11

You descended from heaven like a dove, rested on Jesus, and have remained on Him since the day John baptized Him.
John 1:32-34; Matthew 3:16

Led by You, Holy Spirit, Jesus entered the wilderness. Over the course of forty days of fasting, He faced temptations from Satan.
Luke 4:1-2; Matthew 4:1-2; Mark 1:12-13

Jesus returned to Galilee filled with your power, Holy Spirit, and news about Him spread throughout the surrounding region.
Luke 4:14

It was You, the Spirit of the Lord, Who anointed Jesus to proclaim good news to the poor, freedom for the prisoners, recovery of sight for the blind, liberation for the oppressed, and to announce that the time of the Lord's favor has come.
Luke 4:18-19; Isaiah 61:1-2

It was through You, Holy Spirit, that God anointed Jesus with power to go about doing good and healing all who were oppressed by the devil, because God was with Him.
Acts 10:38

Jesus was filled with your joy, Holy Spirit, when the seventy-two returned, reporting that even the demons submitted to them in His name. Jesus declared, 'Father, thank You for hiding these things from those who think themselves wise and clever, and for revealing them to the childlike. Yes, Father, it pleased You to do it this way.'
Luke 10:21, 17

Holy Spirit, when an individual comes to Jesus, believes in Him, and drinks, they receive You—streams of living water flowing out from within them.
John 7:37-39

You, Holy Spirit, rest upon Jesus—the Spirit of the Lord, the Spirit of Wisdom, Spirit of Understanding, Spirit of Counsel, Spirit of Might, the Spirit of Knowledge, and the Spirit of the Fear of the Lord.
Isaiah 11:2

God placed You upon Jesus to proclaim justice to the nations.
Matthew 12:18; Isaiah 42:1

Generously and without measure, You, Holy Spirit, were poured out on Jesus as He spoke the words of God.
John 3:34

At the final moment before Jesus' death on the cross He cried out, 'Father, into your hands I entrust My Spirit,' yielding His Spirit before breathing His last.
Luke 23:45-46; Matthew 27:50-51; Mark 15:37-38; John 19:30

Through You Holy Spirit, Christ was raised from the dead.
Romans 8:11

Jesus was put to death in the body but made alive in You, Holy Spirit.
1 Peter 3:18

By You, Christ was vindicated.
1 Timothy 3:16

Through You, the Spirit of Holiness, Jesus was appointed the Son of God with power by His resurrection from the dead.
Romans 1:4

Jesus appears to His disciples after His resurrection showing them His hands and His side saying, "Peace be with you …" Then He breathed You onto the disciples saying, "Receive the Holy Spirit."
John 20:19-22

The Prophet Joel (approx. 2700 years ago) declared that You, the Spirit, would be poured out on all people.
Joel 2:28

Jesus promised to send You, Holy Spirit, and told His disciples to stay in the city until clothed with your power from on high.
Luke 24:49

Jesus insists that His disciples should wait for You, the Gift, and that after a few days they would be immersed in You.
Acts 1:5

He also said that when You, Holy Spirit, come upon them, they will receive power, and be His witnesses, even to the ends of the earth.
Act 1:8

It was fulfilled when You came suddenly from heaven with a sound like a violent wind, filling the entire house where 120 believers were gathered. They witnessed what appeared as tongues of fire, separating, and resting on each of them. You, Holy Spirit, filled them all, empowering them to speak in other tongues.
Acts 2:2-4

After receiving You, the disciples were accused of being drunk. But Peter told the crowd, "These men are not drunk as you suppose. No, this is what was spoken by the Prophet Joel: 'In the last days, God says, I will pour out My Spirit upon all people. Your sons and daughters will prophesy, and young men will see visions, your old men will dream dreams. Even on my servants, both men and women, I will pour out my Spirit, and they will prophesy.'"
Acts 2:15-18; Joel 2:28-29

Peter proclaimed that it was You, Holy Spirit, who was poured out on 120 believers on the day of Pentecost.
Acts 2:33

Peter, filled with You, addressed the teachers of the law explaining that he had healed the lame man by the name of Jesus Christ.
Acts 4:8-12

When the believers were praying together, the place was shaken, and it was You, Holy Spirit, who filled all of them, empowering them to speak the Word of God with boldness.
Acts 4:31

Stephen, filled with You, looked up to heaven and saw the glory of God, and Jesus standing at the right hand of God. While they were stoning him, Stephen prayed, "Lord Jesus, receive my spirit."
Acts 7:55, 59

O Holy Spirit, You instructed Philip, "Go over to that chariot and walk along beside it." As Philip ran up to it, he heard the Ethiopian court official, a eunuch serving the queen of Ethiopia, reading Isaiah 53. Philip shared the Good News of Jesus with him. The official believed and was baptized by Philip on the spot. After they emerged from the water, You, Holy Spirit, snatched Philip away, and he found himself at Azotus (approx 20 miles away).
Acts 8:29-30, 35, 38-40

While Peter was speaking, You, Holy Spirit, fell upon all who were listening, and they began to speak in tongues and praise God. Peter exclaimed, "They have received the Holy Spirit just as we have! Can anyone withhold water for baptizing these people?"
Acts 10:44-46

After the vision revealed that what God has cleansed should not be called impure, symbolizing the inclusion of non-Jews, now considered clean and welcomed to receive salvation, You, Holy Spirit, encouraged Peter not to hesitate. You urged him to accompany the men to Caesarea and share with the Gentile household that they, too, can receive salvation.
Acts 11:9-14

When Peter addressed the Gentiles in the household, You, Holy Spirit, fell upon all of them. Peter exclaimed, "God has given them the same gift He gave us (the Jews) who believed in the Lord Jesus." He then recalled how John baptized with water, but they would be baptized with You, the Holy Spirit. Thus, God accepted the Gentiles into the faith, granting them the privilege of repenting and receiving eternal life.
Acts 11:15-18

When Paul laid hands on them (about 12 men), You, the Holy Spirit, came upon them, and they spoke in tongues and prophesied.
Acts 19:6-7

Paul taught that anyone who speaks in a tongue utters mysteries in You, the Spirit. They are not speaking to men, but to God, because no one understands them. He who speaks in a tongue edifies himself.
1 Corinthians 14:2, 4

In his letter to the Corinthian church, the Apostle Paul explains that when he prays in a tongue, it is his spirit praying, but his mind is unproductive [because it does not understand what the spirit is praying]. Therefore, Paul says he will pray with his spirit (in tongues) and also with his understanding. He will sing with his spirit (in tongues) and sing with his understanding.
1 Corinthians 14:14-15

You, Holy Spirit, prevented Paul and Silas from preaching the word in Asia, so they traveled onward. When they reached the border of Mysia and attempted to enter, You, the Spirit of Jesus, did not permit them. Consequently, they journeyed to Troas. One night, Paul had a vision of a man from Macedonia pleading, "Come over to Macedonia and help us." Responding to this call, Paul and Silas went to preach the gospel there.
Acts 16:6-10

You, the Spirit, compelled Paul to go to Jerusalem, though he did not know what would happen to him there.
Acts 20:22

You, Holy Spirit, appointed overseers to watch over the church of God.
Acts 20:28

You fill believers with yourself and with Fire.
Matthew 3:11; Luke 3:16

During the era of the initial tabernacle, access to the Most Holy Place was exclusively granted to the high priest just once a year. He entered bearing the blood of animal sacrifices for both his sins and those of the people. However, these sacrifices failed to purify the consciences of the people. By this arrangement, You, Holy Spirit, made it clear that the way into the present accessible Most Holy Place in heaven could not be revealed while the original tabernacle was still standing.
Hebrews 9:7-9; Leviticus 16:2-22

But through You, the Eternal Spirit, Jesus, our High Priest entered the Most Holy Place—the perfect tabernacle in heaven. There, He offered himself, His own blood, once and for all, to cleanse the worshiper's conscience from all sin and secure their redemption forever.
Hebrews 9:11-14, 7:27

You, the Spirit, testify that God grants eternal life through the Son of God.
1 John 5:7-8, 11

Holy Spirit, You convict the world of its sin, and of God's righteousness, and of the coming judgment.
John 16:8

It was in You, the Spirit, that the Apostle John received his prophetic visions when on the island of Patmos.
Revelation 1:9-11, 4:2, 17:3, 21:10

It is through You, the power of the Spirit of God, that the Gospel is preached, and that signs and wonders and miracles are performed.
Romans 15:19-20

You are restraining (holding back) the Antichrist until the Day of the Lord.
2 Thessalonians 2:2-3, 6-7

It is through You, the breath (Spirit) of the Lord Jesus' mouth, that the man of lawlessness (the antichrist) will be destroyed at the majesty of the Lord's arrival.
2 Thessalonians 2:8

You, the Spirit, convey to the church that whoever overcomes will be granted the right to eat from the tree of life in the Paradise of God.
Revelation 2:7

11

WHO HOLY SPIRIT IS TO ME

You are the gift given to me when I believed in the Lord Jesus Christ.
Acts 11:17

Jesus breathed You on me saying, "Receive the Holy Spirit."
John 20:22

It is You, Holy Spirit, I received when I first repented.
Acts 2:38

When I asked, the Father in heaven gave You to me.
Luke 11:13

Holy Spirit, God caused You to dwell within me, and He passionately desires that You in me remain faithful to Him.
James 4:5

You are my Helper (Advocate) that Jesus asked from the Father, who abides with me and in me forever.
John 14:16-17

You, Holy Spirit, are the gift promised to me and to my children.
Acts 2:38-39

You are my Paraclete (called to my aid, helper, legal advocate, comforter).
John 14:26, 16:7

Holy Spirit, I know You, for You remain with me, and You are in me.
John 14:17

It is by You, Holy Spirit, that I can say, "Jesus is Lord."
1 Corinthians 12:3

Through You, God pours His love in my heart.
Romans 5:5

You, the Spirit of Jesus, reside in my heart, urging me to cry out, "Abba, Father (Dad, Papa)," because I am His beloved son/daughter.
Galatians 4:6

You, Holy Spirit, reside within me. My body is God's temple, with You as its sanctuary.
1 Corinthians 3:16-17, 6:19; Ephesians 2:22

You are within me through the work of God.
Ezekiel 36:26-27

You are my living water.
John 4:10-11

You are streams of living water flowing out from my innermost being.
John 7:38-39

You, in me, are a fountain of water springing up
to eternal life.
John 4:14

If You, the Spirit, reside in me, I am able to accept
and understand the things that come from You and
will not consider them foolish, because they are
spiritually discerned.
1 Corinthians 2:14

You are the power of my witness for Christ.
Acts 1:8

You, living within me, are more powerful than
the spirit in those of the world. Therefore, I have
already prevailed.
1 John 4:4

You empower my inner being with God's
strength, allowing Christ to dwell in my heart.
Ephesians 3:16-17

Holy Spirit, you are writing a letter from Christ on
my heart, not with ink, but with your living
presence.
2 Corinthians 3:3

You, the new Spirit dwelling within my heart of
flesh, have inscribed God's law on my heart,
making me one of God's people.
Ezekiel 11:19; Jeremiah 31:33

You are the new Spirit within me that replaced my
stubborn heart with a heart eager to obey God's
laws and teachings.
Ezekiel 36:26-27

You are the One bearing witness to the Covenant
that God's laws are in my heart and inscribed on my
mind, that my sins are no longer remembered
because of Jesus' sin offering.
Hebrews 8:10, 10:15-18

Holy Spirit, because I have been born of You and
of water, I have seen, entered, and now inherit the
Kingdom of God.
John 3:3, 5-7

It is by You, the Spirit, and not by might or by power.
Zechariah 4:6

If I am led by You, the Spirit, I am not under the law.
Galatians 5:18

If You live in me, I am no longer controlled by
my sinful nature, but by You, the Spirit.
Romans 8:9-10

My spirit (the spirit of man) is the lamp of the Lord,
searching the inner depths of my heart.
Proverbs 20:27

God searches my heart and understands your (the Spirit's) thoughts and purposes because You intercede for me in alignment with God's divine will.
Romans 8:27

You, Holy Spirit, bear witness with my spirit (the spirit of man) affirming that I am God's child.
Romans 8:16

You empower me to remain in God's love as I strengthen myself through prayer, growing in my most sacred faith.
Jude 1:20-21

Holy Spirit, You want me to plant in your field, gathering the harvest of eternal life from You, instead of planting in the field of my selfish desires, which leads to the harvest of destruction.
Galatians 6:8

You do not want me to get drunk with wine, but be filled with You, the Spirit.
Ephesians 5:18

In You, Holy Spirit, the kingdom of God is characterized by righteousness, peace, and joy—not centered on eating and drinking. This allows me to serve Christ, be pleasing to God, and approved by people.
Romans 14:18

In the last days, mockers will follow their ungodly desires, devoid of the Spirit. They cause divisions, but by praying in You, Holy Spirit, I build myself up in faith and remain in God's love, awaiting Jesus' merciful gift of eternal life.
Jude 1:18-21

Through You, I eagerly receive by faith the righteousness that God has promised to me.
Galatians 5:5

As I trust in Him, may the God of hope fill me with joy and peace, so that I will overflow with hope by your empowering presence, Holy Spirit.
Romans 15:13

You, the Spirit, and I, together say, "Come Lord Jesus!"
Revelation 22:17, 20

12

WHAT HOLY SPIRIT DOES FOR ME

You made me. You are the breath from the Almighty
Who gave me life.
Job 33:4

You give me life.
John 6:63

Holy Spirit, You give me access to the Father through
Jesus.
Ephesians 2:18

You are my gift from God.
Acts 10:45

Upon receiving You, Father God adopted me, and You,
Holy Spirit, bear witness with my spirit that I am God's
child.
Romans 8:15-16

Guided by You, I am a child of God.
Romans 8:14

You have come to guide me into all truth.
John 16:13

Holy Spirit, You produce this type of fruit in my life: Love, Joy, Peace, Patience, Kindness, Goodness, Faithfulness, Gentleness, and Self-Control.
Galatians 5:22-23

In Christ Jesus, You, the life-giving Spirit, set me free from the power of sin that leads to death.
Romans 8:2

Through You, Holy Spirit, I am being renewed and am saved through the washing of new birth.
Titus 3:5

By You, Holy Spirit, and in the name of the Lord Jesus Christ, I am cleansed, made holy, and justified.
1 Corinthians 6:11

God placed His seal of ownership on me by putting You, Holy Spirit, in my heart as a pledge guaranteeing my inheritance to come.
2 Corinthians 1:22, 5:5; Ephesians 1:13-14

You seal me for my day of redemption.
Ephesians 4:30

By faith I receive You, the promised Spirit, so that the blessing of Abraham can come to me through Christ Jesus.
Galatians 3:14

I am baptized with water, and baptized with You, Holy Spirit.
Acts 1:5

You baptize me with yourself and with fire.
Luke 3:16; Matthew 3:11

You clothe me with power from on high.
Luke 24:49

You do not want me to extinguish You or scoff at prophecies, but test everything.
1 Thessalonians 5:19-21

Holy Spirit, You search out everything and show me God's deep secrets.
1 Corinthians 2:10

You know God's thoughts.
1 Corinthians 2:11

You know my thoughts.
1 Corinthians 2:11

You are the One Who helps me understand what God has freely given me.
1 Corinthians 2:12

Through You, I speak in a tongue to God, uttering mysteries through the Spirit within me. Speaking in tongues edifies me. Praying in tongues is my spirit praying. Singing in tongues is my spirit singing. Blessing in tongues is my spirit giving thanks.
1 Corinthians 14:2, 4, 14-17

Since the law of Moses was unable to save me because of the weakness of my sinful nature, God did what the law could not do. God sent His own son in a body like mine. And in Jesus' body, God declared an end to sin's reign over me through His son's sacrifice. This was done to fully satisfy the righteous requirement of the law in me, enabling me today to follow You, the Spirit. Now I can live by your way and set my mind on the things that please You, Holy Spirit. This is how I follow You instead of my sinful nature.
Romans 8:3-5

You, Holy Spirit, call me to live by You and walk in step with You, and since I belong to Christ Jesus, I have nailed the passions and desires of my sinful nature to His cross and crucified them there.
Galatians 5:24-25

You, the Spirit, and my flesh are opposed to each other. Therefore, You desire that I choose to walk in step with You, aligning with your guidance, to avoid fulfilling the sinful desires of my human inclinations.
Galatians 5:16-17

You pray for me.
Romans 8:27

Holy Spirit, You intercede on my behalf with wordless groans helping me in my weakness; for I am often unsure of what to pray for.
Romans 8:26-27

You fellowship with me.
2 Corinthians 13:14; Philippians 2:1

You teach me all things and remind me of everything
Jesus said.
John 14:26; Luke 12:12

You, Holy Spirit, make known to me what You receive
from Jesus, thus glorifying Him, for all that belongs to
the Father also belongs to Jesus.
John 16:14-15

Holy Spirit, You speak whatever You hear from your
Father and announce it to me, for You do not speak on
your own authority.
John 16:13

You tell me about my future.
John 16:13

You lead me.
John 3:8; Romans 8:14; Galatians 5:18

You call me to make every effort to preserve the unity
of believers through the bond of peace. For there is one
body and one Spirit, one Lord, one faith, one baptism,
one God and Father of all.
Ephesians 4:3-5

You unite me with other members of the
body of Christ, with Jesus as the head.
1 Corinthians 12:27; Ephesians 4:3-4

For by You, one Spirit, we were all baptized into one body (the Body of Christ), and were all made to drink of You, the one Spirit.
1 Corinthians 12:13

It is through You, the Eternal Spirit, that the High Priest, Jesus, entered the Most Holy Place, the perfect tabernacle not made with human hands. There, He offered himself, His own blood, one time, to cleanse my conscience, sanctify me, and secure my eternal redemption so that I may worship the Living God!
Hebrews 9:11-14

Holy Spirit, I will live according to your guidance, not yielding to my sinful nature, and I will keep my mind set on what You desire, for the mindset of the flesh leads to death, but your mindset is life and peace.
Romans 8:4-6

This, I can use to discern the spirits and determine their origin: Any spirit not confessing that Jesus Christ came in a human body is not from God.
1 John 4:2-3

You, the Spirit of Glory, rest on me when I am insulted for bearing the name of Christ.
1 Peter 4:14

With prayer and petition, in You, Holy Spirit, I pray at all times and on every occasion.
Ephesians 6:18

You help me in my weakness.
Romans 8:26

You, the wind/breath of God, lift up a standard against my enemies.
Isaiah 59:19

It is your sword, the Word of God, that I wield.
Ephesians 6:17; Hebrews 4:12

You, the Spirit, are being poured out on my descendants. Some of them will write the Lord's name on their hands.
Isaiah 44:3, 5

You, the Spirit, remain with me. I am not afraid.
Haggai 2:5

You provide me with power, love, and self-control, not fear and timidity.
2 Timothy 1:7

Because You have testified of Jesus, I too am compelled to testify of Jesus.
John 15:26-27

Finally, I focus my thoughts on what is true, and honorable, and just, and pure, and lovely, and commendable—all that is excellent and worthy of praise. May the God of peace be with me.

Philippians 4:8-9

13

THE IMPACT OF SPEAKING
THE DECLARATIONS

Proclaiming God's truth transforms your life in profound ways. In this chapter, I explore five key benefits of vocally declaring from the 800+ declarations, as opposed to merely reading or silently reciting them in your mind.

It Accomplishes His Purposes

Do you want God's will in your life? Do you want Him to activate you to fulfill what He's called you to do? Do you want Him to shape you into who you're meant to be? If so, declare His words and watch what happens.

> *So is My Word that goes out from My mouth: It will not return to Me empty but will accomplish what I desire and achieve the purpose for which I sent it.* (Isaiah 55:11, NIV)

You see, when you align your words with God's words and cooperate with Him, He fulfills His will in you and through you, accomplishing His purpose. Can you trust Him to know what's best for your life? Then align your words with who He says He is and what He promises to do in you and through you.

> *You will also declare a thing, and it will be established for you; so light will shine on your ways.* (Job 22:28, NKJV).

> *Praise the Lord, you his angels, you mighty ones who do his bidding, who obey His word* (Psalm 103:20, NIV).

Angels are agents of God's word, commissioned to fulfill God's will. When you proclaim God's written promises in faith, you align with His will, prompting divine and angelic action.

It Strengthens Your Faith

When you speak the declarations aloud, you anchor your faith in God's Word, deepening your trust in His promises.

> *Faith comes from what is **heard**, and what is **heard** comes through the Word of Christ* (Romans 10:17, NRSV).

The word "heard" appears twice in this passage, underscoring that faith grows when you hear yourself proclaiming God's Word.

> *So let the one who has My Word **speak** it faithfully* (Jeremiah 23:28, NIV).

By faithfully speaking these Scripture-based declarations, your confidence in God becomes stronger, leading to a steadfast faith that emboldens you to believe for greater things.

It Has Creative Power

God's spoken Word created the universe and all it contains. He spoke, and it became reality. Similarly, Jesus' words brought miracles, healing, and freedom, for He is unchanging, yesterday, today, and forever.

> *Jesus reached out and touched him. "I am willing," he said. "Be healed!" And instantly the leprosy disappeared* (Matthew 8:3, NLT).

> *Jesus Christ is the same yesterday, today, and forever* (Hebrews 13:8, NLT).

> *God calls into being things that are not* (Romans 4:17, NIV).

When you faithfully proclaim God's promises aloud, you unleash His creative power to bring physical healings, salvation to loved ones, and open doors of opportunity that you thought were closed.

It Defeats the Enemy's Plans

When you proclaim the Scripture-based declarations aloud, you wield God's Word like a hammer, shattering the enemy's schemes and silencing his lies. By speaking His truth, you dismantle spiritual strongholds and claim victory in Christ.

> *"Is not My Word like a fire?" says the LORD, "And like a hammer that breaks the rock in pieces?"* (Jeremiah 23:29, NKJV).

In the wilderness, Jesus confronted Satan's temptations three times responding each time with *"It is WRITTEN,"* and quoting Scripture aloud (Matthew 4:4, 7, 10). His spoken Word crushed the enemy's plans.

> *I have given you authority to trample on snakes and scorpions and to overcome all the power of the enemy; nothing will harm you* (Luke 10:19, NIV).

Jesus empowers you with this authority today. Identify your specific struggles—distraction, worry, fear, anxiety, condemnation, depression, temptation, infirmity, or other struggles. Now fill in the blanks below, and assertively proclaim the following declaration now:

> "Jesus, You have given me the authority to trample on snakes and scorpions and to overcome all the power of the enemy. In Your mighty name, I command the spirits of _____ and _____ to leave me now!"

Through steadfast proclamation of His truth, you defeat the enemy's plans, standing firm in Christ's victory.

It Ushers in God's Peace

When you declare these declarations aloud, you find comfort in times of trouble and uncertainty, ushering in a peace that transcends understanding and calms your anxious heart and mind.

> *I have told you these things, so that in Me you may have peace. In this world you will have trouble. But take heart! I have overcome the world.* (John 16:33, NIV)

Jesus speaks these words to His disciples, assuring them that in Him they *can* have peace. Jesus says to you right now, "In Me you can have peace." Pause and experience His presence within you. He takes pleasure in who He made you to be. Allow His peace to wash over you as you daily declare His words.

> *Whatever is true, honorable, just, pure, lovely, commendable — if anything is excellent or praiseworthy, think about these things. Practice these things, and the peace of God will be with you.* (Philippians 4:8-9, ESV, paraphrased)

Speaking Scripture shifts your thoughts from problems to Jesus' presence and peace. Because He and His Word are true, honorable, just, pure, and commendable, when you declare His words, you become aware of His presence within you. This awareness brings refreshing peace that steadies your soul and spirit in His love.

In summary, daily declaring God's Word and these declarations will fortify your future, family, relationships, work, finances, and health. God wants to unleash His creative power, strengthen your faith, defeat the enemy's plans, and bring His divine peace.

14
DIRECT ACCESS TO GOD
Biblical Support for a Divine Encounter

No matter what is happening in your life, no matter how you feel—whether you're on the mountaintop or in the valley, whether your circumstances are great or whether they're cruddy, whether you feel close to God or far away—rest assured that you can boldly enter His presence and receive personal ministry from Him right now.

These foundational biblical truths stated below are crucial in building the confidence necessary to embark on this life-changing journey. It is essential to grasp that, as a believer, you have a remarkable inheritance.

You can confidently step into God's presence, all thanks to Jesus' sacrificial act.

- **Tearing of the Curtain**—More than 2,000 years ago, during the crucifixion of Jesus, something extraordinary happened within the Jewish temple. A thick curtain stood as a barrier between common folk and the Most Holy Place (Leviticus 16:2-3), regarded as God's primary earthly dwelling. However, at the precise moment of Jesus' death, this curtain was miraculously torn in two, from top to bottom (Matthew 27:51; Mark 15:38; Luke 23:45).

- **Removal of the Barrier**—Hebrews 10:20 (ESV) provides a profound insight: We can enter the holy place "…by the new and living way that He opened for us through the curtain, that is, through His flesh." This verse indicates that when Jesus' flesh was torn, the curtain in the temple was torn, enabling you to come face to face with God, who is now your Father. This profound event removed the barrier between humanity and God allowing you direct access to Him anywhere, anytime.

- **Forgiveness through Repentance**—If you confess your sins, God is faithful and just to forgive you and cleanse you from ALL unrighteousness (1 John 1:9). This cleansing occurs the moment you confess; then you are immediately deemed holy and blameless in His presence (1 John 1:7; Colossians 1:22).

- **Guilty conscience cleansed**—Your heart has been sprinkled with Christ's blood, cleansing you of your guilty conscience (Hebrews 10:19-23).

- **Sins Removed and Forgotten**—He chooses to place every sin as far away as the east is from the west (Psalm 103:12), and to remember them no more (Hebrews 8:12).

- **Righteousness in Christ**—You have become the righteousness of God because God made Jesus to be sin on your behalf (2 Corinthians 5:21). Let that sink in. When God sees you, He approves of you because you are a bearer of Jesus' righteousness. You are justified in God's sight. It is not earned; it is given through exchange. Christ became sin, and in exchange for your sin, you receive His righteousness. You cannot buy righteousness; it has already been paid for.

- **Sympathetic High Priest**—This High Priest of yours (Jesus) sympathizes with your weaknesses and invites you to come confidently to God's throne of grace to receive His mercy and find His grace to help you in your times of need (Hebrews 4:15-16).

- **His Return**—He will come again, not to bear your sin, but to bring salvation to all who are eagerly awaiting His return (Hebrews 9:28).

With these foundational truths in mind, take a bold step toward accessing your Father's presence, made possible by Jesus' sacrifice!

The next few chapters introduce a daily practice that will usher you into His presence, allowing you to experience divine encounters and foster an ever-deepening, experiential relationship with each member of the Triune Godhead.

THE DECLARATIONS

15
10 STEPS TO A DIVINE ENCOUNTER – QUICK GUIDE

Guideline for a 20–30 Minute Daily Practice

Consider addressing God, Jesus, or the Holy Spirit on different days, alternating to deepen your relationship with and to clearly hear from each One of Them.

1. Praise Him from the "Who He Is" chapter: Spend 3–4 minutes declaring portions of His names and attributes.

2. Thank Him from the "What He Does" chapter: Spend 3–4 minutes declaring portions of what He does. Insert "Thank You" at the beginning of some of them.

3. Praise Him from the "Who He Is to Me" chapter: Spend 3–4 minutes declaring portions of these personalized declarations.

4. Thank Him from the "What He Does for Me" chapter: Spend 3–4 minutes declaring portions of what He does for you. Insert "Thank You" at the beginning of some of them.

5. Thank Him in your own words: Spend 2–3 minutes declaring what He has done for you personally that has positively impacted your life, whether recently or in the distant past.

6. Confess sin: Ask Him if there is any sin you need to confess. If sins are revealed, promptly confess them and receive His forgiveness before proceeding.

7. Forgive: Ask Him to reveal anyone, including yourself, whom you need to forgive. If someone comes to mind, promptly extend forgiveness before moving forward.

8. Encounter and Commune: Verbally ask Him one of the following, then pause to listen: "What is your word for me today?" "What are You declaring over me?" "Who do You say I am?" "What do You want me to know?" Or ask any other personal question.

9. Journal: Write down the personal insights He shares with you. Then, ask Him to elaborate on what He just said, or pose a follow-up question.

10. Declare back to Him: Rephrase the insights He just shared, writing them in the first person, then speak them out loud as affirmations and remain open to more dialogue with Him.

Call to me and I will answer you, and will tell you great and hidden things you have not known.
(Jeremiah 33:3, NRSV)

To receive a free one-page download of the
"Quick Guide: 10 Steps to a Divine Encounter",
visit www.TheDeclarations.com

16

10 STEPS TO A DIVINE ENCOUNTER – IN–DEPTH

These steps build upon the "10 Steps to a Divine Encounter–Quick Guide," offering detailed insights into the 'why' and 'how' behind each step. This in-depth guide is designed to roll out the red carpet towards the Lord's presence, ensuring you can approach and interact with Him freely, without any obstacles.

Aim to follow these steps daily. Reaching the 'Encounter & Commune' stage takes about 20 minutes, but allow 30 minutes or more for a deeply meaningful, unhurried conversation with the Lord.

To make this process easier, visit my website to print the free '10 Steps to a Divine Encounter–Quick Guide,' which keeps the instructions handy without flipping between Chapter 15 and the declaration chapters, or scan the QR code on page 222 to download the guide.

To begin, locate a calm and quiet place without any possible distractions. If your home tends to be noisy, you might want to consider investing in headphones to block out any background sounds. I highly recommend silencing your cell phone and muting all notifications. This block of time is exclusively reserved for your connection with the Lord.

Consider dedicating specific days to focus your

attention on God, some days on Jesus, and other days on the Holy Spirit. On occasion, intermingle your devotion, praising all three members of the Trinity. Varying your approach enriches your understanding and deepens your connection with each Person of the Trinity, encouraging a more in-depth relationship.

While speaking the declarations is both enjoyable and impactful, limiting your time on Steps 1–4 is crucial to ensure ample opportunity for an experiential encounter with the Lord. Suppose this particular day you want to focus on Jesus. It is not necessary to declare *all* of Jesus' Scriptures in Steps 1–4 as you need to save time for Steps 5–7. Consider using a timer or stopwatch, dedicating only 3 to 4 minutes for each of Jesus' 4 declaration chapters. By following a 20-minute timeline for the first 7 steps, you ensure, again, ample time to connect with Jesus in Steps 8–10, listening for His voice, journaling what you hear, and responding to Him.

You do not always need to begin at the start of each chapter. For instance, in Step 1, you might start at the beginning of 'Who Jesus Is', but in Step 2, you could recite the declarations on every other page of 'What Jesus Does.' In Step 3, you may want to start in the middle of 'Who Jesus is to Me,' and in Step 4, you may opt to speak every third or fourth declaration of 'What Jesus Does for Me.' The key is to be led by the Holy Spirit in navigating through those 4 chapters, remembering to keep to the 3–4-minute timeframe for each. For easy navigation while flipping to various chapters, consider adding tabs where each declaration chapter begins.

Even if certain declarations do not immediately

resonate with you, voice them anyway instead of skipping over them, because every declaration has the power to awaken your spirit, shifting your focus from yourself to Him.

As you use the '10 Steps,' personalize them as you wish, for example:

Use terms like Papa, Father, Dad, Abba, or Daddy interchangeably at the beginning of some of the 'Who God Is to Me' or 'What God Does for Me' declarations.

Use terms like Lord, Savior, Master, Friend, or Brother interchangeably or place your hand on your heart when declaring 'Who Jesus Is to Me' or 'What Jesus Does for Me.'

Walk, joyfully shout declarations, or raise your hands towards heaven when declaring 'Who God, Jesus, or Holy Spirit Is.'

Place your hand on your belly when declaring 'Who Holy Spirit Is to Me' or 'What Holy Spirit Does for Me.'

Step 1: Praise Him for Who He Is

Praise involves extolling, expressing approval, and showing admiration through vocalization, beyond just silent contemplation or reading of His praises. This practice should not be confined to a once-a-week church service or limited to being done solely with music and lyrics. Praise is a vital part of a life surrendered to God, and the main reason we do it is because He is more than deserving; He is absolutely and infinitely worthy of our **praise**.

> *I will praise you, Lord, with all my heart; I will tell*
> *of all the marvelous things you have done. I will be*
> *filled with joy because of you. I will sing praises to*
> *your name, O Most High* (Psalm 9:1-2, NLT).

God understands that when we offer praise, and our attention shifts toward Him, it is immensely beneficial for us. It is in our very nature to praise and worship God, and as we do so, we find our greatest fulfillment.

Speaking the declarations of the character of God, Jesus, or the Holy Spirit is a form of praise and an acknowledgment of who They are. Devoting time to praise is essential for nurturing an intimate and interactive relationship with Them. Instead of simply reciting the declarations, it is important to proclaim them while visualizing and reflecting on the words that describe Their attributes and physical presence.

> *Enter his gates with thanksgiving; go into his courts*
> *with **praise**. Give thanks to him and **praise his***
> ***name*** (Psalm 100:4, NLT).

Through praise, you openly acknowledge His divine nature and your own humanity. Praise aligns everything in the right perspective each day. Using *The Declarations* is a wonderful way to offer praise to God!

Step 2: Thank Him for What He Does

There is a progression. After praising Him, declaring Who He is, it is time to thank Him. Use the list from *The Declarations* titled 'What God, Jesus, or the Holy Spirit Does.'

Scripture-based thanksgiving declarations direct your attention to what the Godhead **does**. And genuine thanksgiving automatically puts the spotlight on Him, not yourself or your needs. But do not worry, They will pour into you and meet your needs at Step 8.

As you declare the deeds God has done and thank Him, you invite His active presence into your life. One way He operates is by thwarting the plans of your enemy, just as God did with the armies of Ammon and Moab at Mount Seir! Satan hates you talking about all the wonderful things God has done, is doing, and is going to do.

> *As they moved forward ahead of the army, they sang, "**Give thanks** to the Lord, for His love endures forever!" The instant they began to **shout and give thanks**, the Lord arranged a surprise attack against their enemies, causing them to turn on one another and suffer defeat. When the men of Judah surveyed the scene, they saw a vast multitude of dead bodies on the ground* (2 Chronicles 20:21-24)

Each day, dedicate a few minutes to focus on a member of the Trinity. Express gratitude by preceding some verses with "Thank You" as you recite them aloud. You will witness how this practice can be a powerful tool to silence anxiety and worries.

Step 3: Praise Him for Who He Is to You

These declarations tell God "This is Who You are to me," not "This is who I am" or "This is who I am to You." Nearly all the declarations begin with "You," referring to one of the members of the Trinity. These declarations always focus on Him, not ourselves. For example, 'You are my Savior' versus 'I am saved.' The former emphasizes His personal relationship with you, while the latter primarily reflects your identity, lacking the depth of personal bond with you. Also, notice that saying 'You are my Savior' directs your attention to Him and His personal connection with you, whereas saying 'I am saved' shifts your focus to yourself.

This may seem subtle, but it is crucial to view everything from God's perspective of us—how He sees us, who He is to us—rather than who we are to Him. The best way to accomplish this is by reading, meditating on, and declaring from His Word and from these declarations who He is to you and what He does for you, then listening to what He has to say to you personally.

> . . . he (Abraham) grew strong and was empowered by faith as he gave praise and glory to God (Romans 4:20, AMPC).

Following the example of Abraham, your faith will be fortified when you first verbally praise God for

Who He Is. Then, and only then, praise Him for Who He Is to you.

If you can grasp this concept, you will realize that who you are to God is not as important as who God is to you. Example: If you tell God the Father, 'I am your son/daughter,' the focus is still on you telling God who you are to Him. If you instead tell God, 'You are my heavenly Father,' you are telling God who He is to you. It's fine to declare both, but Who He is to you should take precedence over who you are to Him.

This is why the declarations do not start with the words, 'I am.' Although 'I am' decrees are valuable, God desires to go beyond these. He wants to speak to you directly and tell you who you are. After He tells you who you are to Him in an encounter, then yes, you can declare those words He just told you, back to Him as affirmations. And yes, they will be 'I am' statements but they are birthed out of an interactive exchange between you and God, receiving direct words from God in real-time. This is priceless, and far surpasses the act of merely uttering 'I am' affirmations.

We will explore this further when I explain Step 8 through 10.

Step 4: Thank Him for What He Does for You

Utilize the list of declarations titled 'What God, Jesus, or the Holy Spirit Does for You.' Precede some of the paraphrased Scriptures with "Thank you."

> *… in every situation, by prayer and petition, <u>with thanksgiving</u>, present your requests to God. And the peace of God, which transcends all understanding, will guard your hearts and your minds in Christ Jesus* (Philippians 4:6-7, NIV).

This set of declarations tells God, "This is what You do for me." While it may appear self-centered, it still puts the spotlight on Him and serves as a powerful affirmation that God is actively involved in your life. He not only wants to be but delights in it, and these declarations act as strong reminders that He indeed is active in your life.

Step 5: Thank Him in Your Own Words

Now take a couple of minutes to thank Him out loud for those moments when He directly impacted your life. Thank Him for His patience when you were stubborn, for His presence during your hospital stay, or for His help when you faced job loss. Thank Him for those personal, private moments between just you and Him. Relive those times with Him, sharing how much you value His role in those specific situations. Recall the promises He has already fulfilled in your life and express your gratitude.

> *Be thankful in all circumstances, for this is God's will for you who belong to Christ Jesus.*
> (1 Thessalonians 5:18, NLT)

Certain memories will forever hold a special place in your heart, and you will thank Him for them throughout eternity. However, it is beneficial to vary the things you are grateful for each time you give thanks, deepening your bond with Him. If you ever find yourself running out of past stories to be thankful for, ask Him to bring new ones to mind. Trust Him to jog your memory. You can also express gratitude in advance for what you hope and believe He will do in your future. This act of thanking God in advance reflects your faith and brings Him joy because He delights in hearing words of faith from you.

Step 6: Confess Sin

Ask God if there are any sins you need to confess. If nothing immediately comes to mind, there is no need to forcefully dredge up something. Proceed to the next step.

If sins do come to your awareness, promptly ask for forgiveness for them. As clearly explained in Chapter 14, know that as soon as you confess, God faithfully forgives, immediately covering your sins with His Son's blood, and never recalls them again.

> *In Him we have redemption through his blood, the forgiveness of sins, in accordance with the riches of God's grace* (Ephesians 1:7, NIV).

> *He has removed our sins as far from us as the east is from the west* (Psalm 103:12, NLT).

After confessing, if you find yourself struggling with feelings of guilt and unworthiness, it is time to command the spirit of self-condemnation to depart in Jesus' name! Speak aloud to rebuke it, then forgive yourself for the confessed sin. Strengthen your faith by reciting more 'Who God is to You' and 'What He Does for You' declarations. Once done, proceed to Step 7.

Step 7: Forgive

Simply ask the Lord if there is anyone you need to forgive. If a name comes to mind, just say, "I forgive _____(name)," and move on. This also includes forgiving yourself.

I realize that this is easier said than done. So, before we delve into the process of forgiveness, let us address some common but incorrect views. Some believe forgiveness is optional, dependent on feelings, or that it requires trust and/or reconciliation. Others may think forgiving someone means condoning their actions, or that forgiveness should only be extended after receiving an apology. But these misconceptions can hinder the path to true forgiveness.

Forgive others—
Forgiveness is not optional; it is a command from God.

All four Gospels emphasize that forgiving others is essential for receiving God's forgiveness. Jesus made it clear that if you want to be forgiven by God, you must also forgive others (Matthew 6:14-15; Mark 11:25; Luke 6:37; John 20:23).

Forgiveness is not about your feelings; it is a deliberate choice. It does not mean ignoring the hurt caused, excusing, or condoning the offense. No. Forgiveness is about letting go of the grudge and releasing others from the blame. If the pain persists, continue choosing to forgive, while seeking God's healing for those wounds.

> *Do not take revenge, my dear friends, but leave room for God's wrath, for it is written, "It is mine to avenge, I will repay," says the Lord* (Romans 12:19, NIV).

Forgiveness does not equal trust; we are commanded to forgive but not necessarily to trust indiscriminately. We can place trust in the Lord while extending forgiveness to those who have not earned it.

Forgiveness does not necessarily mean reconciliation; it involves extending forgiveness even in cases where reconciliation may not be possible.

> *If it is possible, as far as it depends on you, live at peace with everyone* (Romans 12:18, NIV).

Notice Scripture says, "**If** it is possible, . . ."

Forgiveness does not let the offender off the hook; it means we can and should still hold others accountable for what they do or what they fail to do.

You do not need to wait for others to ask for forgiveness before you forgive. And you do not always have to tell them you have forgiven them. Announcing forgiveness to someone who has not asked for it may come across as self-righteous.

Forgive yourself—
If you are burdened by guilt, forgive yourself. You may believe something from your past was your fault, and you may think that you do not deserve freedom. However, it is important to release thoughts of self-punishment and put the sin and your mistakes as far away as the east is to the west, just as God does when He forgives you. Rely on God's boundless love and mercy captured in the words of this Psalm.

> *He does not deal with us according to our sins, nor repay us according to our iniquities. For as high as the heavens are above the earth, so great is his steadfast love toward those who fear him* (Psalm 103:10-11, ESV).

Forgive God—
Although God cannot sin and does not require forgiveness, holding unforgiveness towards Him can be a challenging ordeal. This often stems from your belief that God has either remained passive, allowed suffering, or played a role in your hardships. Waiting for, or demanding answers from God before extending forgiveness, can hinder your healing journey.

A positive approach would be to address God directly, saying, "Lord, I choose to forgive You, despite not fully understanding why this has happened in my life. I acknowledge my dilemma does not alter your fundamental goodness, love, or justice. By choosing this, I let go of my need for immediate answers and trust fully in Your divine wisdom and plan."

As you approach the encounter stage, let us take a moment to recap your journey: You have dedicated 3 to 4 minutes each to declaring 'Who He Is,' then 3 to 4 minutes on 'What He Does,' followed by 3 to 4 minutes expressing 'Who He Is to You,' and then 3 to 4 minutes on 'What He Does for You.' If you add an extra 2 or 3 minutes to thank Him in your own words, and about 2 minutes for confessing sins and forgiving, that totals approximately 20 minutes. Now, you are prepared and ready to hear from the Lord!

Step 8: Encounter and Commune

For this step, have a pen and paper, a journal, or a device ready to record what you hear from God.

Begin by asking God just one of the following questions, and listen carefully for His response:

> *"What is your word for me today?"*
> *"What are You declaring over me?"*
> *"Who do You say I am?"*
> *"What do You want me to know?"*
> *"Who am I to You?"*
> …or ask any other personal question.

Listen carefully, accepting the first response with trust, open to His voice. Having offered Him the praise He cherishes most, He now seeks to offer you the personal intimacy you value most.

Remember Jesus' words:

Whoever belongs to God hears what God says. I am the good shepherd; I know my sheep and my sheep know me. My sheep listen to My voice; I know them, and they follow me" (John 8:47, 10:14, 27, NIV).

Each of us is uniquely formed, designed to recognize His voice when He speaks. We *can* know His voice. The key is to rely more on His ability to get through to you than on your own ability to hear Him. He wants us to be confident in hearing from Him.

How precious to me are your thoughts, God! How vast is the sum of them! Were I to count them, they would outnumber the grains of the sand—when I awake, I am still with you (Psalm 139:17-18, NIV).

God's thoughts toward you are constant and countless, more numerous than the grains of sand. With such an abundance of care, doesn't it follow that He desires you to align with His heart and hear His voice? Do Jesus and Holy Spirit also cherish you, longing for you to receive Their thoughts and know Their love? Consider this example: If the Lord says, "I love you," ask

Him, "What do you love most about me?"

Your personal communion with the Trinity is Their deepest desire, a relationship with you, interaction with you. They use each moment of your genuine personal connection with Them to transform you into Their image.

> *The Lord… makes us more and more like him as we are changed into his glorious image* (2 Corinthians 3:18, NLT).

I was guiding a man over the phone through the '10 Steps,' with his copy of my book in hand. At Step 8, he asked God, "What do You want me to know?" He heard, "I'm proud of you." He was deeply moved by this simple affirmation from Him and could have stopped there, content with God's words. But I encouraged him to ask a follow-up question, though he struggled to think of one. I suggested he build on His words by asking, "What are You most proud of about me?" Many find it hard to receive praise from the Lord, but he asked, and this is what he heard: "I'm proud of your steadfast heart, always seeking My purpose for your life." He paused in silence, taking it all in.

After a moment, I encouraged him to continue with this question: "Is there anything else You want me to know?" God responded, "I'm also proud of how you represent Me well at your workplace."

He journaled God's words (Step 9–10) and spoke them back to Him: "Father, You're proud of me. You value my steadfast heart, always seeking your purpose for me. You're proud that I represent You well at my workplace." God always has more to share, but often He pauses to let you reflect on His words. This man was greatly encouraged by what he heard, especially as his first conversation with Him. I knew he was ready to use these steps daily to hear from God on his own.

God's personal words not only edify us, but instruct and teach us the truth. He also enlightens us about our faults, guiding us towards righteousness.

> *All Scripture is God-breathed and is profitable for instruction, for conviction, for correction, for training in righteousness* (2 Timothy 3:16, AMP).

The Holy Spirit is your Advocate. He teaches you and reminds you of Jesus' teachings.

> *When the Father sends the Advocate as my representative—that is, the Holy Spirit—he will teach you everything and will remind you of everything I have told you* (John 14:26, NLT).

He guides you into the truth.

> *When he, the Spirit of truth, comes, he will guide you into all the truth* (John 16:13, NIV).

He gives you messages of knowledge as well as discernment.

> *The Spirit gives… a message of special knowledge … by the same Spirit… the ability to discern whether a message is from the Spirit of God or from another spirit…* (1 Corinthians 12:8,10, NLT).

By pausing and listening attentively, you will receive personal instruction, messages, correction, knowledge, discernment, clarity, and even engage in dialogue with Him.

When you reach Step 8, confidently ask, "Lord, who do You say I am?" without fearing His reply. By daily declaring 'Who God Is,' 'What He Does,' 'Who He Is to Me,' and 'What He Does for Me,' you will know Him more and like Peter, He will show you who you are in Him and what He calls you to do.

Jesus posed the question:

> *"Who do you say I am?" Simon Peter answered,*
> *"You are the Messiah, the Son of the living God."*
> *Jesus replied, "And I tell you that you are Peter,*
> *and on this rock I will build my church, and the*
> *gates of Hades will not overcome it. I will give you*
> *the keys of the kingdom of heaven, and whatever*
> *you loose on earth will be loosed in heaven."*
> (Matthew 16:15-16, 18-19, NIV)

As you declare His character and works, He reveals who you are in Him and your calling.

Now let us explore what it is like to hear from God.

Individuals experience God's communication in a variety of ways. Some people hear His words internally, like an inner knowing, often described as, "I just know in my knower what He is saying to me." Others say they receive something in their spirit that resembles a voice and are certain they have heard something. This is sometimes referred to as the voice of peace. Others call it hearing things spiritually. Some may see images forming in their mind's eye, or their spiritual eyes. For others, God expresses Himself as a strong impression, similar to intuition. Yet others sense a Scripture or a song echoing within them. It is crucial to pay attention, as these experiences are very likely God expressing Himself to you.

As you explore these varied experiences, remember that discerning His voice is a learned skill. The more you engage the '10 Steps to a Divine Encounter', the more you will become familiar with the variety of ways He makes His thoughts and desires known to you. Yes, He will correct you at times, but it is always done with respect and love.

If you do not *hear* anything during the initial days of practicing the 10 Steps, don't be discouraged and stay persistent. Your breakthrough will come. Again, place greater trust in God's ability to communicate with you than in your own ability to hear Him.

Learn to listen to Him. When you believe you've heard from Him, write it down and repeat it back to Him—say what He just said about you. Don't just think it, say it. Then ask Him to elaborate on what He has just spoken to you. Get the conversation going. If He says something you don't quite understand, ask Him, "What do You mean by that?"—just like you would with a friend who said something unclear. Once you feel comfortable hearing from Him and responding to Him, you'll be amazed at how much He enjoys you! Learn to fellowship with Him—this is an art.

Step 9: Write down the personal insights He imparts to you.

It is important to document what God says, as doing so helps you reflect, contemplate, and more fully absorb what He has revealed.

> *Write down clearly on tablets what I reveal to you, so that it can be read at a glance* (Habakkuk 2:2 GNT).

I keep a Word document titled 'My Fellowship with the Father, Jesus, and Holy Spirit.' Over the course of a year, this document has grown to approximately 50 pages (12-point font). It includes messages from Them, my responses, scriptural studies, reflections, personal struggles, and victories.

> *My son, pay attention to my words, and listen closely to what I say. Do not let them out of your sight; keep them within your heart. For they are life to those who find them, and healing to their whole body.* (Proverbs 4:20-22, ISV)

Keep a journal, whether written in notebooks, digital, or audio format, and review it often to place Him and what He says at the forefront of your thoughts. This practice also guards your heart and keeps you connected, accountable and submitted to God.

Step 10: Personalize His words, declare them back to Him in the first person, and remain open to a dialogue.

I have briefly touched on the beauty of fostering fellowship with each member of the Trinity by asking questions, documenting Their answers, and becoming familiar with hearing from Them. Now, I'd like to provide additional tips on deepening the encounter.

In the first nine steps, you initiate the conversation by verbally praising Him for who He is, thanking Him for what He does, and acknowledging who He is to you and what He does for you. You then allow Him to wash away any sin that can hinder your fellowship, and you release any grudges toward those made in His image. After asking Him a question, He naturally responds, and you write it down in Step 9.

As mentioned earlier, God is looking for a response from you, much like a friend waiting for you to reciprocate. The best way to respond is by aligning yourself with what He has just imparted. Take a moment to prepare what you will say back to Him.

For example, if you heard God say the following to you in Step 8: "Stay attuned to My Spirit throughout the day. You have not been outside of My will in the last couple of days, as you presume. Do not doubt this, and you will see wonderful things happen."

Simply copy and paste, or rewrite, the exact words He spoke in your journal, switching 'you' to 'I,' 'I' to 'you,' and 'My' to 'Your,' adding words as needed for clarity.

Here is an example of how you can respond to God: "I will stay attuned to your Spirit throughout the day. I have not been outside of your will in the last couple of days as I presumed. If I do not doubt this, I will see wonderful things happen."

Note the last sentence God said: "Do not doubt this, and you will see wonderful things happen." Here, He is offering a conditional promise—if you come into agreement with Him and reject the lie that you have been disobedient these past days, you will witness wonderful things. Often, God will highlight areas of your life that need to be addressed to help you break negative behavioral, emotional, or thought patterns.

So, don't be surprised if God adds more to the conversation, providing you with insights and strategies to overcome strongholds. If He does, keep writing and keep responding! Every moment you spend in dialogue with the Lord, whether frequent or rare, is significant. These exchanges, no matter how brief or long, contribute to a deeper, more meaningful relationship with Him. As you align yourself with His words and respond, you open yourself up to further insights and affirmations from God.

17

MY DIVINE ENCOUNTERS

Next, I want to share with you two firsthand accounts of my experiences with the '10 Steps to a Divine Encounter.' I will guide you through each step, detailing my dialogue with God and Jesus, and how I echoed His words back to Him during our devotion time. These notes are directly extracted from my Word document, recorded as I engaged in these personal encounters.

Sometimes He shares brief, comforting phrases, and at other times, these conversations extend into deep, loving, corrective teachings. These exchanges bring conviction, drawing me closer to Him and prompting me to delve deeper into Scripture to better understand the truth He reveals.

Example 1: Today I'm speaking God's declarations.

Step 1: After approximately 3 minutes of speaking about 25 declarations from 'Who God Is', I'm struck by how great and caring He is.

Step 2: After 3 minutes of uttering 25 declarations from 'What God Does' and adding "Thank You" in front of several of them, I am already starting to forget about my problems.

Step 3: After dedicating 3 minutes to proclaiming 20 declarations from 'Who God Is to Me', I am encouraged by His unwavering faithfulness to me.

Step 4: After dedicating 3 minutes to vocalizing 20 declarations from 'What God Does for Me', adding "Thank You" to about half of them, I am struck by the extent to which God is for me.

Step 5: At this moment, I am experiencing a profound sense of peace and appreciation. I express gratitude to God for specific blessings, speaking aloud: "Thank You, Father, for providing the strength to complete this book, for the provision that covered the recent unexpected car repairs, for the wonderful fellowship with my friends the other day, for keeping me from getting discouraged when thinking about the world's challenges, and for continuously inviting me into your presence."

Step 6: I am in a moment of reflection, asking God to reveal any sins I need to confess. Two come to the surface: "Please forgive me for neglecting our fellowship over the past couple of days due to busyness. I also ask for forgiveness for my impatience with my husband today."

Step 7: Now, Lord, show me who I need to forgive. Today, only one name comes to mind. I whisper, "I forgive (name)."

Step 8: I asked God, "What is your word for me today?"

Step 9: This is what I journaled about the experience: Suddenly, an overwhelming purity washes over me as I am drawn into His presence. I become acutely aware of God's holiness. It strikes me how unworthy I am to be in the presence of such holiness. My immediate response is to draw back, thinking, "I'm not worthy." But in this very moment, Jesus steps forward, extends His scarred wrists, and whispers, "You are not worthy. No one is. That is why I did this. Come close."

I am consumed by His profound love and His yearning for intimacy. Tears flow freely as I find myself in awe that He knows every aspect of my being—the good, the bad, the ugly—yet He has an unwavering longing to draw near to me.

Step 10: I am going to repeat the following in the first person back to Jesus: "I am not worthy. No one is. You did what You did on the cross so that I can draw close to You."

It is interesting that even though I was focusing on God and His declarations today, Jesus stepped in to address my struggle with unworthiness.

Now, let us move on to another, lengthier example.

Example 2: Today I chose to speak Jesus' declarations.

Step 1: After spending about 5 minutes vocalizing around 15 declarations from 'Who Jesus Is', I find myself captivated by the scriptural paraphrases that describe Jesus' physical attributes and the characteristics of His throne. As I visualize what Isaiah, Ezekiel, Daniel, and John might have witnessed and heard, I am filled with awe at the majesty of Jesus. I never tire of declaring who Jesus is.

Step 2: Now, I am devoting approximately three minutes to uttering 20 declarations from 'What Jesus Does,' adding "Thank You" in front of several of them. For variety, I decided to begin about halfway through the list. As I declare these, I feel incredibly grateful for everything Jesus has done and continues to do.

Step 3: Now, I take around three minutes to declare 20 statements from 'Who Jesus Is to Me'. I start about halfway through this category. Today, I'm realizing a new aspect of Jesus' role—that of a brother to me! We share the same Papa. (Rom. 8:29, Heb. 2:11)

Step 4: I proceed to declare 20 verses from 'What Jesus Does for Me,' starting around midway through this section in roughly three minutes, pausing to express gratitude by prefacing about half of these verses with "thank you."

Step 5: I call to mind specific things for which I am grateful to Jesus, saying, "Thank You for your personal presence in my life, for revealing to me that our time together is the most significant part of my day. Thank you for healing me of cancer in my 20s and in my 30s, and for the privilege of representing You to others throughout my life."

Step 6: I turn to Jesus and ask Him to reveal any sins that need confessing. One thing comes to mind, and I confess, "Lord, I ask for your forgiveness for resisting your guidance and not following your promptings to work on certain tasks over the past several days. I have been feeling like a failure in your eyes."

Step 7: I ask Jesus to reveal to me anyone I need to forgive. Today, feeling condemned, I choose to extend forgiveness to myself, saying, "Jesus, I forgive myself, though I recognize I've let You down."

Step 8: **I ask Him:** "Jesus, who do You say I am?"

Step 9: Here is the dialogue between Jesus and me.

Jesus: *Haven't I told you that you are My beloved? I do not judge you. Do not judge yourself. Do you consider yourself a disappointment?*

Me: *Yes.*

Jesus: *Beloved, you have no authority over yourself. My Father and I alone have authority over you, and I am **full** of* *grace. Do not focus on yourself at all. Look to Me. Avoid self-evaluation and self-critique. Let me handle that. My Father alone judges and evaluates righteously, and He does not keep record of what you call failures. Only you do that.*

Me: *Okay, Lord, how do You evaluate me?*

Jesus: *I see a compassionate daughter, sister, friend, and mother. I see someone struggling to meet her own expectations. You are not allowed to have self-imposed expectations. I am cleaning you out while you are working on this book. Even though you do not see progress, everything I am doing inside of you during the process is part of being a good steward of Our book. (Jesus always begins affirming who you are while delivering a corrective word.)*

Me: *So, I cannot look back over the last few days or weeks and try to figure out why there was no progress on this book?*

Jesus: *NO, YOU CANNOT! The Father has not given you jurisdiction over your past sins or mistakes. You are not allowed to look at yourself and your past through just your own eyes. You have made yourself the judge and the jury. My Father is the Judge on the bench. Look to Me. Look at Me, and ask Me, because I do not condemn you! I want you to resist your temptation to self-evaluate, self-critique, or self-judge in ways that pinpoint your perceived shortcomings and deliver a self-verdict. You are still performance-oriented! (Jesus is giving me a corrective word, but the way He does it is remarkably constructive.)*

Let us look at what you have done over these past

several days. With My guidance and strength, you culled through all the sections of the book that needed attention and arranged them in order of priority. Through My leading, you spoke with some people at Costco and led one of them to Me. In My strength, you served your husband well while he was struggling these past weeks. Through Me, you did much, much more!

If you find yourself tempted to assess or judge yourself or your performance, invite Me to assist you in the evaluation, for you are to acknowledge Me in all your ways. Lean not on your own understanding, and I will direct your path.

*But back to how I see you...I see a powerful woman, loved and cherished by the Father. I see a woman who is focused on pleasing Him. However, she keeps forgetting that He is already pleased with her. She can stop focusing on trying to make Him proud in what she **does** (performing), and, instead, focus on receiving His love and acceptance for **who** she is.*

*I see a daughter who loves My Father with all her might. I see an obedient daughter. Are you able to accept the Father's love and affirmation for **who** you are? Devoting time to Him and turning to Him for guidance fuels your productivity. You are not your own source of motivation. Dedicate time to embrace His daily acceptance, pleasure, and approval.*

Step 10: I am now going to rephrase the insights He just shared, writing them in the first person to declare directly to Jesus.

Below, I have transposed all the 'you' words to 'I,' and all the 'I' words to 'You,' and have reformatted the structure while keeping the content intact.

I say the following out loud to Jesus:

Me: *Jesus, You are reminding me once again that I am your beloved. You do not judge me, so I must not judge myself. I have no authority over myself—You alone have authority over me, and You are **full** of grace.*

You instruct me not to focus on myself and my failures but to look to You and avoid evaluating myself. <u>You</u> want to handle that, for your Father judges and evaluates righteously without keeping a record of what I call failures. I alone have done that.

Here is how You evaluate me today: You see a compassionate daughter, sister, friend, and mother. You see my struggles to meet my own expectations, reminding me that I am not allowed to impose these self-expectations. In my work on this book, even when I cannot see progress, You are cleaning me out as part of the process of stewarding our book.

*Jesus, You say that I **cannot** look back over the last few days or weeks to evaluate my progress without your input. You have not given me jurisdiction over my past sins or mistakes. I have made myself my own judge and jury, but only my Father is the righteous Judge on the bench, and You do not condemn me.*

You insist that I look to You, focus on You, and ask You, because You do not condemn me! You want me to resist the temptation to self-evaluate, self-critique, or self-judge in ways that pinpoint my perceived shortcomings that lead me to deliver a verdict. You say that I am still performance-oriented!

You want me to recognize the work I have done in your strength over the past several days, which includes prioritizing the book's sections, leading someone to You at Costco, serving my husband well during his struggles, and much, much more! When I am tempted to evaluate myself and my performance, I am, instead, to acknowledge You in whatever I am doing and ask for your guidance. I choose to lean not on my own understanding but on yours, and I invite you to direct my path.

You see me as a powerful woman, loved and cherished by my Father, focused on pleasing Him. Jesus, You want me to know that my Father is already pleased with me. I am to shift my focus from trying to make the Father proud of what I do (performing) and instead focus on receiving His love and acceptance for **who** *I am—a beloved daughter.*

Today, You have challenged me to find fuel in your daily acceptance, pleasure, and approval. Yes Lord. Please remind me of the importance of this when I slip into my old ways.

Afterward, I wanted to dig into the Word because these two Scriptures stood out to me.

> *Jesus said to the Pharisees, "You judge according to human standards. I do not judge anyone. But even if I do judge, My judgment is true."*
> (John 8:15-16, AMP)

> *The Apostle Paul wrote, "I do not even examine myself ... the one who examines me is the Lord. Therefore do not go on passing judgment . . ."*
> (1 Corinthians 4:3-5, NASB)

Both Scriptures apply to the lesson Jesus just taught: that examining myself by human standards (judging myself) leads to a performance-based lifestyle. Jesus now forbids me from examining myself (self-evaluating) because I end up passing judgment on myself, which He says is not my jurisdiction. God is the One who judges righteously. Me, as my own judge and jury, will condemn myself every time. Today's lesson is God does not condemn me. I am to stop critical self-evaluation and simply look to Him for His righteous evaluation of me and my work.

18
OTHERS' DIVINE ENCOUNTERS

**Meet lives transformed by pursuing
the '10 Steps to a Divine Encounter' to hear God.**

Cynthia hears God say, "I love you for who you are."

"My mind often swirls with negative thoughts about myself, and I typically turn to Jesus in prayer, rather than God. I had always imagined God up there with a very stern, intimidating, hard look on His face, peering down from His throne. Regardless, I decided to focus on God the Father and try the '10 Steps to a Divine Encounter.' As I followed each step, declaring portions from chapters 1 to 4 to God, not once did I think or feel any negativity toward myself. It was a time of just me and God, and I felt loved by Him.

"As I reached Step 8, the Lord spoke to me, affirming that I am His daughter, that I am kind, and forgiving, that I am peace, and I am healed. He said that He wants me to repeat this practice often, in a quiet place, because I am easily distracted and need to hear Him. And He repeated, 'You need to quiet yourself and listen for Me.' I promptly wrote all this down. When I reached Step 10, concerning the things He told me, I declared them back to Him. In that moment, I discovered He is actually a really cool Dad! I distinctly heard Him say 'I love you no matter what you've done,' while smiling and adding, 'There's nothing wrong with you.' This brought a feeling of hope and peace to my heart. I realized I do not need to define myself. I also heard Him say, 'I love you for who you are, and who I created you to be.' What a wonderful Father He is!"

Gideon hears God say, "I'm always here for you."

"For years, I felt distant from God, wrestling with insecurities and hurts from family and past relationships. Without being secure in His love, I fell into addictions. Then, a friend introduced me to the "10 Steps to a Divine Encounter' in *The Declarations*. As I declared the verses about who God is in me and for me, I felt welcomed, not judged, and realized how far I'd strayed. God's words became clear, saying 'I'm always here for you. You don't need to earn My approval. You don't need to strive to hear Me. I'm the God of restoration,' … and more. Through these encounters, He's healing my wounds and filling me with wisdom and encouragement. I'm closer to Him now, back in church, and thankful for this amazing journey."

Kathy hears God and journals conversations

"I would hear God's voice from time to time, but my spirit longed for more, restless for deeper connection. In 2023, the Lord told me, 'Just listen to Me.' That year, I waited eagerly for His voice, but the conversations I desired, didn't come. When a friend gave me your book and I read an example of your dialogues with God, I found hope. After using the '10 Steps to a Divine Encounter' following the simple explanations, I began getting half to three-quarters of a page of personal dialogues with God daily! Now, nearly every week, I meet up with others to help them encounter God using the '10 Steps.' What an incredible ministry!"

Evelyn hears Jesus say, "You will be healed!"

"My sister gifted me *The Declarations* book when I began to face a dire prognosis with a baseball-sized cancerous tumor blocking my bladder, causing unbearable, agonizing level 8-10 pain for months and months. Chemo and radiation failed, and doctors offered little hope, emphasizing the tumor's persistence on MRIs. I lived with a catheter draining urine into an exterior bag through a hole near my belly button, which caused continual bacterial infections. Despite this, my faith grew through the '10 Steps to a Divine Encounter,' which I practiced consistently, alternating my focus to Jesus, the Holy Spirit, or God the Father. This deepened my personal connection with them, giving me hope and reinforcing each One's love and care for me.

"For months, my sister guided me through the '10 Steps' via phone calls many times, taking notes of my conversations with God, feeding me His rephrased words for me to verbally affirm back to God in the first person. Part of what Jesus told me, about the 10th time we did this was, 'Cast out the spirit of despair. You do have hope for a future. You will be healed!' As I repeated, 'I cast out the spirit of despair. I do have hope for a future. I will be healed!' I started vomiting and continued speaking the rest of Jesus' words between puking. I knew my healing was happening!

"The next day, I had my scheduled MRI. Four days later, my oncologist was stunned, viewing the MRI and palpating, saying the tumor had vanished and the lymph nodes were fine. I audio-recorded our conversation of her exclaiming 12 times that it was gone! She said I'd be able to urinate normally now. It's been a year since the miracle, and I'm still speaking the declarations, continually experiencing God's goodness."

Kathy leads group to hear God's voice

"I frequently guide individuals over the phone, and occasionally groups in person, through the '10 Steps to a Divine Encounter.' Recently, I was thrilled to lead a group of ten young adults enrolled in a ministerial course at our church through this process. After we declared the first four steps together, we proceeded through steps five, six, and seven with a sense of anticipation. For step eight, I invited them to write down the question, 'Father God, who do You say I am?' and to listen quietly for His response, recording what they heard.

"After giving them time to reflect and write, I asked if anyone wanted to share. The students were pleasantly surprised by the clarity of God's voice. Three men shared along the lines of God confirming their calling to ministry. The women, visibly moved, revealed that God spoke to their hearts about their true worth and value. The 10-Step process was remarkably effective, enabling students—many lacking confidence—to hear God's personal words and encounter His voice in a profound, unexpected manner. I'm overjoyed at how God works through me to touch people's lives."

TESTIMONIES OF PEOPLE SPEAKING THE DECLARATIONS

15-Minute devotion to one Person of the Trinity

"I've always valued my connection with Holy Spirit, but I've found new insights I hadn't explored before. Today, I spent three to four minutes reading Holy Spirit's attributes and workings from each of Chapters 9 through 12 in *The Declarations.* This structured approach led me to revisit the declarations and their linked Bible verses, which clarified key truths. Studying and reflecting on them has sharpened my understanding of who Holy Spirit is, what He does, who He is in me, and how He works through me. This practice deepens my walk with Him, revealing His guidance daily."

Engaging family Bible study

Every Saturday morning, my wife, our two teenagers, and I gather for our Bible study, proclaiming declarations from *The Declarations*. We choose a member of the Trinity to honor each week, and each of us speaks for exactly three minutes in turn. For example, if we focus on Jesus, I start with 'Who Jesus Is,' my wife follows with 'What Jesus Does,' our son shares 'Who Jesus Is to Me,' and our daughter declares 'What Jesus Does for Me.' We often switch roles for variety.

"Afterward, we share which declarations resonated, reading the corresponding Bible verses. We tie these Scriptures to what's going on in our lives, which gets the kids talking about their struggles, connects us to God, and keeps every gathering fresh with Scriptures that speak to us. I encourage every family to speak these

declarations together and study God's Word as we do—
you'll see Him move in amazing ways!"

Using declarations in devotional meditation

"I have been using *The Declarations* during my
devotional and contemplative meditation time, soaking
in His promises and amazing love for me. This is a
weighty book and not something just to read but more
of a practice for life. I'm still lingering in Chapter 2!"

Proclaiming declarations for spiritual warfare

"On every long road trip, my friend and I carry *The
Declarations* book, pausing at state capitols and
courthouses along our route. Facing each building from
its front steps, we pray fervently for revival and take
turns boldly proclaiming from 'Who God Is,' 'Who
Jesus Is,' 'Who Holy Spirit Is,' and chosen declarations
from chapters 2, 6, and 10. We cast off anything that sets
itself up against the knowledge of God and invite God's
Presence, Justice, Wisdom, and solutions to transform
our national, state, and local governments."

Declarations as God-focused worship

"Each morning, I cannot wait to speak the declarations
because He truly does respond. Through this book, I
have learned that when you tell Him who He is, He will
tell you who you are. I've yet to discover another book
like this one, which turns all focus towards Him, God.
Unlike many devotional and declaration books that
center on us, this one is entirely God-focused. I literally
experience a personal revival every day. It's priceless!"

Family Bible study

"My kids, who are 12 and 14, and I, use *The Declarations*

for our family Bible study, starting with Chapter 1 and reading the declarations together. So far, they've worked through Chapters 1–8, looking up Scriptures as we go. They love it! As a parent, I can't be more excited about them enjoying digging into God's Word."

Using declarations to enhance prayer

"As usual, I have various needs and concerns that I always want God to address in prayer. But I've realized that it's better to speak some of the declarations first. Proclaiming His names, character, and expressing gratitude automatically ushers me into the throne room! Surprisingly, I often find that this alone brings such peace that I do not feel the need to ask for anything. It's reassuring to know that I can simply approach Him without constantly wanting something from Him."

Finding peace through declaring God's glory

"Elaine received devastating news from her doctor: she had late-stage cancer and less than a couple of weeks to live. Bedridden at home, she received visits from many family members and friends during her final days. Three of her sisters, including me, devoted a couple of hours each day sitting with her, taking turns speaking the declarations. Personalizing the declarations by inserting her name made it deeply intimate and comforting for Elaine. We coined this practice *The Declarations* Ministry.

"Every time we ministered the declarations, it felt as though the glory of God filled the room. As the Lord nourished her spirit with His words, her feelings of hopelessness and despair began to fade. She remarked that, despite reading her Bible daily for years, she had not been aware of so many characteristics of God.

Profound statements would escape her lips, revealing deep truths. Perhaps she caught a glimpse of heaven because right before she passed, she exclaimed, 'You don't know what you are missing! There's an ocean of wonders about God you have not known!' She also uttered other revelations like 'Jesus is the Origin of Life.' A family member noted that Elaine's expanded understanding of God better prepared her to meet Him.

"Not only was Elaine impacted by hearing the declarations, but everyone within earshot was also affected. One relative saw a vision of Elaine in perfect health standing next to her bedridden body, as if God were revealing Elaine's near-future heavenly state."

Rapid declaration as worship

"Sometimes when I proclaim all of 'Who Jesus Is' declarations rapidly, I sense a surge of God's presence wash over me! The fast-paced back-to-back rhythm unleashes His power and glory in my life. Other days, I do the same with 'Who God Is' and 'Who Holy Spirit Is.' What an exhilarating spiritual rush it is to see, read, and speak Their attributes pouring forth one after another after another!"

Men's Group Bible study

"Our men's Bible study group enjoys *The Declarations*, growing closer to God and each other. Weekly, I assign a different guy to pick a short section of declarations and give a 10-minute talk on his insights, including Bible verses. Sharing prompts lively group discussions. These discussions fuel our hunger for God's Word and deepen our connection with Father God, especially for those with strained earthly father relationships."

Encountering Holy Spirit's power

"I decided to read aloud chapter 10 of *The Declarations*, titled 'What Holy Spirit Does,' in one sitting. Toward the end, during the last 10 to 15 minutes, something extraordinary happened. My entire body began to tremble uncontrollably as I continued speaking the declarations! The shaking persisted for about an hour. Trusting God had been my theme for the year, and through this experience, I felt God's presence so profoundly that I truly understood what it means to trust in Him."

Growing personally & prayer declarations over others

"Each day, I proclaim the declarations from *The Declarations* as I'm led. Every time, it shifts my mind into admiration and praise for God, Jesus, and the Holy Spirit. Solutions to my problems come to me when reading, and peace flows over me every time. This book has transformed me in ways I cannot explain. I also like to declare these verses over my loved ones during my personal prayer time."

Using the '10 Steps' to hear God for others

"Sometimes I'll do the '10 Steps' for the purpose of hearing God for what He wants to reveal to other people. I'll ask God, at Step 8, 'Who is on Your heart today, and what are You declaring over them?' A person's name will come to mind, and I just start writing what He shows me. When I hand it to them, they are usually blown away; it was exactly what they needed to hear."

THE DECLARATIONS

Father, I bless every person who makes these declarations. I pray they experience a profound and enriching relationship with You, where their conversations and dialogues with You become powerful and deep.

Jesus, I pray You reveal to each person who You are in them. May they have boldness to step out, explore, and discover what You can accomplish through their lives, whether it be mighty works, inventiveness, providing solutions to the world's problems, creative designs, or influencing positive change.

Holy Spirit, I pray that every individual may come to recognize and embrace your role in their lives. May they receive your precious gifts, manifest your abundant fruit, and know You are interceding through them, advocating on their behalf, leading, and providing invaluable instruction for their lives.

"It is written!"

—ABOUT THE AUTHOR—

LORRAINE LARZABAL

Lorraine Larzabal's journey is a testament to her unwavering faith and dedication to guiding thousands of individuals towards transformative encounters with God. With over three decades of experience, she has tirelessly taught people to discern the numerous ways in which the Godhead communicates and connects with us, leading to profound experiential dialogues with God the Father, Jesus the Son, and the Holy Spirit.

Lorraine's lifelong commitment to faith and healing is marked by vocalizing biblical passages and personalizing healing verses to overcome sickness. She has witnessed the liberating power of reciting the Word aloud to conquer spiritual oppression. Guided by biblical principles, Lorraine has spent years assisting individuals in confronting past traumatic experiences, facilitating their personal encounters with Jesus.

As a worship leader, she loves integrating songs with 'You are' lyrics, directing the worshipers' full attention toward God for a deeper experiential connection.

Born in McAllen, Texas, as the seventh of nine children, Lorraine initially pursued a corporate career in Houston, Texas. However, at the age of 28, her life took a significant turn when she was diagnosed with cancer.

A profound encounter with Jesus became a turning point as she wholeheartedly dedicated her life to Him. This decision not only infused her life with purpose and meaning but also provided her with the faith to conquer cancer. This crucial phase led her to respond to the call of ministry, where she promptly seized the opportunity by joining Youth With A Mission (YWAM).

Lorraine's journey with YWAM included completing the Discipleship Training School, and a life-changing outreach in Jamaica. There, she founded and led the School of Christian Discipleship for three years. She pursued biblical education, graduating from the YWAM School of Biblical Studies in 1990 with expertise in the Inductive Bible study method. Her focus since then has been on the names, activities, roles, and attributes of the Holy Trinity.

Lorraine has led numerous mission outreaches, including missions to China, Cuba, and Israel, demonstrating her commitment to sharing her faith on a global scale and facilitating others to do the same.

Returning to the United States after her YWAM experiences, Lorraine faced and conquered a second bout of cancer. Undeterred, she ventured into entrepreneurship, successfully operating a physician referral service for nine years. Simultaneously, she graduated from the rigorous five-year course at the Entrepreneurial Development Institute in Houston, Texas. Later, she founded and directed a thriving real estate investment business for five years, then brokered commercial real estate deals for a few years.

Upon moving to Hawaii, she established and serves as President and CEO of Accessing Health, and Accessing Freedom. Additionally, Lorraine and her husband Luis embarked on a joint venture, co-founding and operating a small biotech company.

Since 1990, including after her ordination in 2017, she has remained actively engaged in ministry, currently conducting one-on-one prayer encounters in diverse settings, from private spaces to malls, restaurants, and outdoor events. She also takes joy in training others to lead groups in person or virtually to encounter God and hear His voice, using her '10 Steps to a Divine Encounter.'

Lorraine's life story is one of resilience, faith, and a deep commitment to guiding others on their spiritual journeys. Her experiences, teachings, and ministry have touched countless lives and continue to inspire those who seek a closer connection with God the Father, Jesus the Son, and the Holy Spirit.

LorraineLarzabal.com

To receive a free one-page download of the 'Quick Guide: '10 Steps to a Divine Encounter', visit www.TheDeclarations.com or scan the QR code below.

Notes